The Inferno Within

Inspired by the poem *Comedia* known today as *A Divine Comedy: Dante's Inferno*, written by Dante Alighieri in 1320.

Illustrations by Gustave Dore

All by rutger_vos licensed under CC BY 2.0

Dedicated to all who guided me through my passages...my Virgils'

Copyright © 2020 Maggie Pandolfi
All Rights Reserved
ISBN 978-0-578-70085-4

Table of Contents

Introduction 5
Valley of Desolation 13
Virgil 19
    Shamanic Journey Practice 26
  The Golden Thread 30
  The Power of Evolution 33
Vestibule of Hell 37
  Hornets and Wasps 40
    Belief Deconstruction Practice 40
  Maggots and Worms 44
Upper Hell: Circles of Indulged Passion 49
  Circle of Limbo 51
    The Watcher Practice: 54
  Circle of Lust 57
    Simple Emotional Awareness Practice 60
    Emotional Landscaping 62
  Circle of Gluttony 65
    Emotional Release and Flow Practice 72
  Circle of Greed 77
    Projection Practice: 86
  Circle of Wrath 91
    Calling Inner Voices Practice 94
Lower Hell: Circles of Violence and Fraud 101
  Circle of Heresy 103

- Jumping Over the Fire Ceremony 107
- Circle of Violence 111
  - Personal Inventory.......................................117
- Intermission 121
- Circle of Fraud..127
  - Atonement of and by the Word 129
- Circle of Treachery: Hell...................................135
  - Dark Night of the Soul 141
- Purgatorio...153
  - Intuition 159
    - Three Realm Practice................................164
  - Self Love..167
    - Ho'oponopono Practice............................169
- Paradise 173
  - Presence – Awareness Expansion Practice.................178
- Appendix A- 12 Steps of AA 184
- Bibliography...186

Introduction

The forest was filled with stagnant, dank air and I couldn't see through the mist. It was suffocating and thick. There was a distant voice, that was calling my name....with every step, no matter which direction, it seemed it was getting closer, louder. It sounded hoarse and ancient, "Maggie, it's time."

I could feel my fear flood every cell, stealing every space of sanity. It threatened to stop my breath, my heart was racing. I had to get away, but which way? I couldn't find the path, and stumbled through the darkness, tripping over downed branches and through old leafless bushes. I felt the cobwebs drifting across my face and tears stinging my eyes.

"Maggie, it's time."

I woke up sweating, and found myself in a stranger's house, not remembering how I had gotten there, nor where I was. It seemed I was in the midst of paradox, where the moments stood breathlessly still, yet life was lurching, relentlessly headlong forward and out of my control.

For what seemed like the first time in my life, I was completely and resolutely out of control. I had no say about the wave I found myself caught up in. I felt kidnapped and helpless. And, I was.

"Maggie, it's time," echoed in my mind.

In retrospect, that was exactly where I needed to be nearly 14 years ago. I needed to be between worlds, neither of which I would recognize for some time. But, they came to be known to me many years later as the Valley of Oblivion on one side, and Paradiso on the other. I gained understanding of these Worlds, after much wandering between them, which became my journey that I'd like to share with you.

This wandering turned out to be a phenomenal adventure, even though it meant a few trips to Hell and an intimate encounter with Lucifer, 'my' Lucifer. And although I would like to say that sharing the mishaps of my trek might absolve you from taking the same seemingly wrong turns along the way, to save you from this journey, I cannot, nor would I.

For the destination leads nowhere but this very moment and every step and misstep along the way has intrinsically sacred value, value that cannot be earned any other way. These moments in their fullest, are worth every drop of blood, every tear, when you arrive fully. That's if you survive the journey at all.

And, I wish this for you. I wish upon you the utter annihilation and destruction of your world as you know it. I wish upon you the fiery flames of Hell, and the state of total despair that lie in wait for you. I wish for you the journey many call the Dark Night of the Soul.

For it is only through this initiation into your deepest well of anguish, that your Gates of Paradiso become opened unto you. And, I believe that once you find this Eden, that you will relish, in fact, you will love the passages that must be navigated to have arrived.

I am not a professional therapist, nor healer, nor anyone really out of the ordinary. I am a pilgrim on a pilgrimage. I am much like you and everyone else walking this little blue planet, in the midst of an infinitely incomprehensible Universe. And, I've been blessed with the good fortune of having to meet my demons, smell their stagnant breath, see their bloodshot eyes, and slay my dragons.

I intend to attempt a retelling of this menacing expedition, in the hopes that you can find your way to the edge of the Forbidden Forest, within which lies the Gate to the Divine Inferno. And, you choose to enter, all on your own.

My meandering through my Dark Forest has brought me to meet many Guides along the way, and I will share these with you, along with introducing you to the many Demons and

Beasts I've discovered lurking in my Forest. I've visited their caves, drank of their elixir, dared to stare them down, and lived to tell the story.

Along the way, I gathered courage and hopefully some wisdom, albeit very slowly. And more importantly, I gathered up many secrets of the Forest. I've collected them over the years in journals and these have become the talismans of my personal growth pilgrimage. These talismans are the practices that I've experienced, collected, and loved and continue to practice today. They allow me to coexist with the many Beasts of the Forest, and are the amulets that I depend on to fend off the shadows that lurk in the nightfall.

There are many practices that I've included here for you, to assuage some of your meandering, and harken your expedition straight to the soul of darkness. Know this before we embark, I will not steal your pain.

I've culminated eclectic practices from many different teachings, methodologies, and traditions. And, I use them often today, as I've found that although personal growth can be torturous, it can be incredibly liberating. And, I still wander….as often as possible.

Some of the greatest teachers that I have had are storytellers and mythic poets. Every story or myth ever told speaks to us as humans about our human experience and our innate and mortal human condition. This is what draws us to write them, read them, and retell them. Which is how I've chosen to retell mine, by offering you a framework from which to map out the expedition and help somewhat, to navigate the darkness.

Our humanness is relational in its very nature. My adventure relates, as many do, to what is often called the Hero's/Heroine's Journey, the age-old Descent/Ascent voyage. One of the oldest retellings that I know of, and one of the most dramatic and exquisitely artistic is a poem written by a 14th-century Italian poet, Dante Alighieri. He wrote an epic 3-part work, *Divine Comedy*, which is a depiction of his own macabre psycho-spiritual pilgrimage.

The first part, *Inferno*, details his dream journey through Hell, which is depicted as nine concentric circles, each leading deeper into the mystic, shadowy realm. He is guided by the ghost of an ancient Roman Poet, Virgil, through the Circles of Hell, into the passages of Purgatory, and finally to arrive into Paradise.

I choose this allegoric parable because it relates closest to my own journey, in that my 'descent' was not linear, nor a one-time event. My descents grew deeper and deeper the farther I explored, and I continue them today. And, every descent to the next depth is met with some degree of exalted ascent, which for Dante is a series of understandings that build the foundation for the next descent. And much to my surprise, in reflecting back over my own history, I too see that each descent was simply a stepping stone into the next, and not always in precise order, but always in sacred order.

The story is written as an allegory, which means it is full of imagery and symbolism. This allows the reader to draw from it what is meaningful to the reader, from their own perspective. I invite you to do just this, as my story is not, nor could be just like yours. In fact, the steps that I've taken from the Valley of my own Oblivion, to the Vestibule to Hell in the Forbidden Forest, through Hell and into my Paradise, is meant to be different than yours.

However, the methodologies and practices that I discovered, and many of the beasts I've met along the way have been excavated from the same soil as yours. We are all human, and thus, therefore, we share. We share much of our very nature, many experiences, emotions, beliefs, thought patterns, and so on.

I believe also that we are each incredibly unique. However, the closer we live in proximity to our primal state, that which we live in when we live obliviously, the more alike we are. It is when we blossom into our individuation, fully embodied, fully alive, fully aware state, that we begin to shine. This shine comes from our inner connection to that which I call Divine.

We awaken to our Divinity when we expand our awareness, express, and reflect the 'more than matter' part of who we are. This is our spiritual self that, as opposed to religious self, is not inhibited by rules, dogma, nor our acculturated limitations. We move from living as a being of matter, to living as a matter of being. This being is a part of something which is greater than our many selves.

Ultimately, you can decide for yourself what this 'something greater' is for yourself. What I can offer to you is that there will come a time, if you decide to come with me, that you will most certainly meet that 'something greater.' In fact, you will have no choice because once committed, there will be no turning back. Let me say again, emphatically, once you enter the mists, they will not release you and there is no return. With emphasis, I say again, *THERE IS NO RETURN.*

The reward will be more than mere survival, it will be a rebirth of life itself.

The paradox is that the closer we get to Hell, the closer to our Divine nature we are. You can only understand this by making the journey yourself. Do you dare to come with me?

We'll explore all of this because I will do a bit of meandering in the retelling too. I plan on meandering between 14th-century Italian poetry, to very utilitarian practices, and then again through excerpts of my own story.

We'll form bridges between many different concepts. Let's bridge the paths that were scripted by those long ago, with those of our modern, daily lives. Let's create a passageway between Oblivion and Paradise. Let's channel the ancient to the present. Let us renew the conduit between the essence of you, and the essence of the Universe.

I invite you to risk entering the Gateway to Hell, to find your way to the Inferno of the Divine, of your own volition, where your very soul awaits you.

"Furthermore, we have not even to risk the adventure alone; for the heroes of all time have gone before us; the labyrinth is thoroughly known; we have only to follow the thread of the hero-path. And where we had thought to find an abomination, we shall find a god; where we had thought to slay another, we shall slay ourselves; where we had thought to travel outward, we shall come to the center of our own existence; where we had thought to be alone, we shall be with all the world."
- Joseph Campbell, The Hero with a Thousand Faces

The lights dim, and the curtains part...

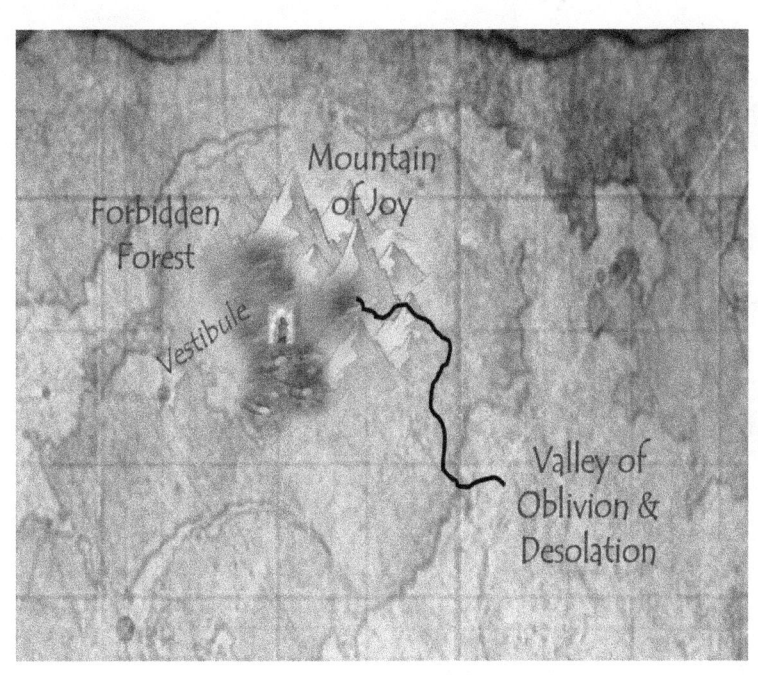

Valley of Desolation

Scarce the ascent
Began, when, lo! a panther, nimble, light,
And cover'd with a speckled skin, appear'd;
Nor, when it saw me, vanish'd.
Canto I., lines 29—32.

And lo! almost where the ascent began,
A panther light and swift exceedingly,
Which with a spotted skin was covered o'er!

He seemed as if against me he were coming
With head uplifted, and with ravenous hunger,
So that it seemed the air was afraid of him;

And a she-wolf, that with all hungerings
Seemed to be laden in her meagerness...

And the time comes that causes him to lose,
Who weeps in all his thoughts and is despondent,

E'en such made me that beast withouten peace,

Which, coming on against me by degrees
Thrust me back thither where the sun is silent 16
                              Dante's Inferno Canto I

Dante's journey begins much the same as many of ours. He has realized that he has strayed from the innocence of his path and is lost in the dark. Out of desperation, he searches for meaning and light, and sets out to climb the obvious, to the Mountain of Joy.

However, along his unsuspecting path he encounters three beasts, the Leopard of Malice and Fraud, the Lion of Violence, and the She-Wolf of Wantoness, who is 'She who steals one's life force.' He must retreat or be eaten alive.

My hope is that you've come to a similar point in your life, where you've found yourself searching, searching for something undefinable, with a knowing that it exists beyond where you live now. You're feeling the urgency to find 'it', as it holds a certainty and promise of more truth, reason, and joy.

And, my hope is that you've found that the path to meaning and joy has been impenetrably blocked, by vile and repulsive beasts threatening your very existence. If you haven't met them yet, I promise you, if you're fortunate, you will...

The origin of the search is reflective of the time that we all face at some point in our lives, where we simply cannot go on living the way we have, and find ourselves lost in the darkness. This can happen to us in many different ways, such as the loss of a loved one, a physical disease or impairment, a nervous breakdown, or an addiction for example. For those lucky few, it may be simply a knowing that there is more to life, but for most of us, it usually takes something nearly catastrophic and has the thick sense of fatality to life as we have known it.

Humans don't change, unless they have to. But when the time comes that change is inevitable, it will feel as though it is a crisis of deathly consequences. It is the Universe offering you a sacred crossroad, where there lie unknown paths, and the always-available retreat to safety.

And the Beasts, well, they are savoring the moment that you must decide and the wrong decision will certainly deliver you into their clutches.

That day came for me on June 26th, 2007, as I awoke in an Alcohol Rehab center, with no clothing except what I was wearing, not even a toothbrush. I had no recollection of how I got there nor where I was. What I did know was that my world, which was my family and work at that time, could not survive without me. I had to get out of there, I didn't belong there and had to get back to where I'd come from.

I met my first of many Beasts to come that morning. My first Beast was Exposure. I had simply been exposed for what I really was, unmasked in front of the world I had so successfully (I thought), kept at bay with my theatrics. I had been 'found out' and my mask of functionality had been ripped from my face. I was splayed before everyone, naked and alone in the darkness.

But my mind worked as it always had...running a well-rehearsed dialogue. I could 'fix' things, just like I'd done a thousand times before.

In reality, I had no idea how to 'fix' anything. When I ventured upstairs on that first morning, I had to face Dr. Judy who apparently, I had met the evening before, but couldn't remember having done so. I did give 'fixing it' a try and attempted to convince her that the world would surely self-destruct if I didn't return to take care of it. I was not 'like them,' and didn't deserve to be here. I was too important. I wasn't a 'drunk.'

Dr. Judy saw beyond the façade of my mask, my rehearsed and habitual script. Her first words to me were so simple yet so profound, "Maggie, it's time. It's time to help yourself."

In stark contrast, I didn't even really know how to do that, let alone take care of anyone else. I, glaringly obvious in this moment, hadn't taken care of anything well my entire life. I needed help to learn what that meant and how to go about it.

But, I needed help?

I fought that idea with every ounce of deceptive energy I had. I fought the idea that the persona I had so successfully created, wasn't real. I fought the notion that I, the great and powerful Oz, hid behind a curtain of deception. I fought the idea that I was an imposter, that I was anything other than a chosen mask for each performance. I fought the Truth.

I believe it was in that moment that I turned back from the Beast of Exposure, and I looked at the path that made its way back down the Mountain and contemplated retreat. What I could see lying in wait at the bottom was a Valley of Desolation.

At first I felt betrayed by whoever had removed my mask and had exposed me. There must be someone to blame. For maybe for the first time in my life though, I heard a stirring from deep inside. It was nearly inaudible, but had the timbre of molten lava, something that was not to be stopped, ignored, or unheard. It grew in insistence, melting the impenetrable rock walls that I had so carefully built around and within me and eventually I could hear, "This is what you've created." I heard, "Maggie, it is time."

I started to glimpse, through the mists of despair, what I had caused to happen in my life. I had been living in the Valley of Desolation, oblivious for so long, thinking that my 'act' and recitation were for others and had magnificently duped my outer world, when in reality, I had duped my inner world. With my oration scripted to conceal some flaw within me, I had wreaked such havoc and drama to my outer world. The curtains were open, and I was exposed.

I had lived there, in my self-constructed Valley of Desolation. And, I had destroyed everything myself, my inner and outer worlds became something completely unrecognizable. The mists grew thicker. The Beasts descended upon me.

But the Beasts were more than the humbling moment of exposure for me. The She-Wolf, as Dante describes her, is the one who steals our life force. It is in this moment of life-changing decision, that we either birth our life force, or we deal it yet another death blow. I chose the former and asked Dr. Judy for help. I had….. surrendered.

I surrendered to possibility.

And I would come to find out that those Beasts had been set upon my path, by none other than myself.

Virgil

Dante in his fear of the Beasts, turns to retreat, and Virgil presents himself....

While I was rushing downward to the lowland,
Before mine eyes did one present himself,
Who seemed from long-continued silence hoarse.

When I beheld him in the desert vast,
"Have pity on me," unto him I cried,
"Whiche'er thou art, or shade or real man!"
                              Dante's Inferno Canto I

You are not alone, you are never alone.

But, you are your own perpetrator, victim, and thankfully, savior.

Dante, in his initial attempt to retreat, is halted by the appearance of the ghost of Virgil, an ancient Roman poet. In Jungian terms, he would be synonymous with our unconscious or higher self. He has appeared to Dante to be his guide to circumnavigate around the Beasts to get to the top of the Mountain of Joy. But, the Mountain of Joy is not as it seems.

Virgil warns Dante that to make this journey, he must take an unbeknownst passage. This passage is hidden well and treacherous beyond comprehension, because there is no easy route to the top of the Mountain of Joy. It is just another illusion. The passage will deliver him to a journey that he has never heard of before, nor ever could have dreamed existed.

He must begin by entering the Dark Forest to find the Gateway of Hell, and then make his way through a travail of repulsion and disgust. Virgil tells Dante that he will, along the way, hear the desperate lamentations of ancient and disconsolate spirits begging for the mercy of their second deaths. And, he must meet great Demons along the way.

Dante is assured however, that the travail is worthy, as Beatrice, who is Dante's long-lost love we learn, awaits him at the other end in Paradise, or in Italian, Paridiso.

As in Dante's tale, I have found that two things most assuredly exist. The first being that many guides avail themselves to you once you have taken the first step of Surrender.

The second and more important is that our deepest desire lies at the end of the unknown path. Beatrice does await at the other end, and much more.

In Dante's story, Beatrice has actually charged Virgil to guide Dante in the hopes that Dante will accept the challenge and find her once again.

Beatrice and Virgil are more like archetypes, which we find in any worthy myth, that of animus and anima. Our animus as I understand it, I think of as more of my inner guide, and my anima as more of my outer guide. We need both when we meet that time in our lives where we are lost and feel hopeless. They are ready to take our hand and lead us gracefully through the challenges that lie still hidden from our sight.

Most stories of this type all contain a character that represents our human consciousness or animus, and another represents our higher, spiritual self or anima. This is Dante's Virgil and Beatrice. And although there are stories where the two begin as adversaries, in this telling, they are compassionate compatriots. Both are vested in Dante's successful completion of his voyage.

When we have come to a point of surrender in our lives, it is not a moment of exasperated giving up, although it can feel that way to begin with. It is a total whole mind/body surrender, to our humanness, our frailty, our imperfections, our beasts. It is the moment in time, when we surrender all of who we have been, not knowing what we will become, not knowing the next act rehearsed ad nauseum till we orate by heart, nor how we can get there.

And when that moment arrives, and you accept the challenge, someone, somehow shows up in your life to lead the way.

Behold the beast, for which I have turned back
"Do thou protect me from her, famous Sage
For she doth make my veins and pulses tremble."

"Thee it behoves to take another road,"
Responded he, when he beheld me weeping,
"If from this savage place thou wouldst escape."

    Virgil represents for us many things. He serves as an Elder who stands by our side as we undergo what lies ahead. He also serves as the animus, the yang of our psyche, or more simplistically, our motivational and primal drive to do what must be done, and go where one must. It is because of meeting Virgil, our animus, that we are curious about what else life holds, knowing that the past cannot be our future any longer.

    And you may ask, was it not him in disguise on the mountain as the Beast? It was my experience that yes, Virgil and the Impassable Beasts were in fact, within, forcing me to look for change, for growth, forgiveness, and to heal.

    Deep in our inner landscape, they have been watchful of our time of implosion expectedly. Ultimately, however, whether or not our Guide(s) come from within or from without, they are our omen of impending doom and hope at the same time.

    Dr. Judy was one of my guides. She was a Native American Elder. I was curious about her beliefs and practices. Interestingly, I had met others just previous to my collapse, who were delving into Shamanic Practicioning as well. These seemed like incoherent coincidences at the time. I would later discover that once I began to wander into the Forest, coincidences would become synchronicities. All of this had some meaning, and I would have some level of understanding, but not until many curtain-calls later.

In the Shamanic Traditions, there is a belief that our guides are always available to us and they come in many forms. They can come for example as Power Animals, Ancestors, Spirit Guides, voices, or Wisdom Fields such as the Akashic.

I was very cynical about these types of beliefs and couldn't fathom that such things were real at this point in my life. After all, didn't all of our strength and intelligence come from our inner ability to power through our outer world?

I began to wonder about my definition of power. I began to wonder about my strongly held beliefs that I was the center of my universe and that I was in control.

What I did know, was that what I knew up to that point, hadn't worked out so well, so why not explore something else? So, humor me, if you are one who is as cynical as I was and venture on a bit further. Maybe all is not as I have always thought it to be.

Given the magnitude of the crossroad at this tie, and the inner knowing that retreat wasn't an option for me, I followed the flow that had been presented to me. I 'trusted' because there was no other choice. Whether or not these extremely foreign people and practices were real or not, I took a risk that the hand that was held out for me to hold, just might be one I could trust.

In retrospect so many years later, it was these hands and so many others that were held out to me, that would hold mine with such Divine guidance.

And ultimately, I would come to understand that it is truly irrelevant whether or not I believed that my guides and my path are an outer interjection by something mystic, or an inner manifestation of my own inner Divinity.

At this stage of life that I had found myself in, I had become *willing to not know*, and this became the elixir of the Chalice that I drank freely from.

Regardless of your beliefs, I invite you to not know.

I invite you to something new and maybe foreign.

I invite you to a Shamanic Journey. The intent is to invite your Guides (inner or outer, it makes no difference right now) to make contact with you, to bring them closer to your active consciousness and begin a relationship with them, in preparation for our pilgrimage.

I invite you to NOT define your 'guide' in any way. Allow it to be your deeper conscience, soul, intuition, or even as many indigenous cultures still teach, our power animals or spirit guides. I invite you to NOT KNOW and simply be curious.

Before we begin, let me offer a bit of explanation to help you if you haven't experienced this before. Shamanic Journeying is an ancient method of inducing a trance-like state that indigenous tribes have used for thousands of years worldwide in rituals. Although it is very different than traditional meditation, it may or may not have a similar intent.

Shamanic Journeying begins by setting a very clear intent and actively engaging some imagination to start. With the assistance of some form of rhythmic induction, the neurological brainwave pattern is synchronized to enter into the Theta state (as opposed to the Delta state where meditation occurs), where we release our practiced thought patterns, and allow for the intention to be played out. When we are in Theta state, we are between being in a relaxed, awakened state, and that of deep sleep.

It is in this light dreaming state, where creativity and inspiration are found. I think of it as a state where the veil is lifted between my human state and my spiritual or sub-conscious state and I become able to travel between the two, yet not dreaming fully or asleep.

The rhythmic induction can be done by the playing of didgeridoos, rattles, rainmakers, singing bowls, or more commonly, drumming, and this is what we will be using. The reason I choose drumming is that our relationship with rhythm begins in the womb, when we are around 20 days old. At around that time, our single 'heart' cell awakens with its first beat, which awakens the cells nearby and they begin to beat with the same rhythm, and a heart is formed. We are serenaded by this same beat from that day to our last. We are innately 'tuned' to rhythm and the drum is the closest instrument to this spectacular phenomenon.

For this practice and others, I have made available a DVD to help facilitate your experience. On that DVD, you will find the Shamanic Journeying chapter, which includes 20 minutes of drumming starting with a short section for guiding you into the Journey.

Let's set our intention to meet our Guide(s). In a relaxing atmosphere, where you won't be disturbed for at least an hour, you would lie down comfortably and start playing the Shamanic Journeying section of the DVD or another drumming audio (these can be downloaded from the internet as well). Make sure that if you do use a download, you obtain an audio specifically meant for Shamanic Journeying, as it is important that the rhythmic pace and changes are correct.

Also, please read through the practice before doing it to familiarize yourself with it.

Shamanic Journey Practice

- Begin with a few minutes of relaxation and deep breathing.
- State your Intention clearly, three times. For example, "I want to meet my Guides."
- As the drumming begins, bring your imagination to a place in nature, where you find comfort and beauty, where you are most likely to find yourself. This is called your Launching Spot.
- Observe the scents around you, the colors, the temperature, the sounds you hear, take it all in. Actively engage as many somatic senses as you can.
- State your intention again.
- Now, <u>engage your imagination</u>, look around you and begin to look for an opening, an opening into somewhere else, into the next world. It may look like a door, mist, hole, pond, ladder, anything. Listen for it, it will tell you it is the door that awaits you.
- Enter that opening, that doorway.
- (From here, you are to release your imagination and simply let go…..)
- (The drum will beat for some time, and when it changes beat, that will be your signal to come back the same way that you came)
- (You will be guided back into a relaxed and conscious state).
- Once awakened, journal everything you can remember, because it will leave your memory quickly as your mind returns to its normal Beta state.

Even though it took you no more than a minute or so to read this, as with all practices I present, they are all meant to be done very slowly, with adequate time for experience. I recommend that you use the DVD for this and all practices so that ample time is taken to do the practice correctly.

Much of this practice is not guided by you or anyone else. It is meant to be this way, so that what needs to happen, will.

Some beginners have a difficult time with different parts of this at first. For example, some can't seem to find the doorway. It may appear as many things, so look without any pre-judgments of what a door should look like. Many tribes use ladders as their doors, such as the Mangar tribe in Nepal and the Dudun of Borneo.

For me when I first experienced this, I came back with a fair dose of cynicism. I believed that what I had just experienced, was pure imagination, or maybe a dream to some degree. And, I tried it a few more times anyhow.

It was the third Journey I took, which gave me reason to start to question my cynicism though.

One woman who was lying next to me began to retell her experience. Halfway through, when she was describing how she had met with a flock of noisy crows who turned out to be protecting her, I was stunned. I too, had had an experience of a crow who had been trying to 'break-in' to my Journey and I had had to chase it away to preserve 'my journey' as I thought of it then.

At first, I thought this was just a coincidence, until it continued to happen nearly every time after that and still does today. Somehow (and frankly, I still have no damn way of explaining this), I engage and see parts of others' Journeys at the same time that I am experiencing my own. Why, I am not sure and still awaiting that answer, but given its nearly 100% recurrence, I no longer can be skeptical.

And, more importantly, I did meet guides. Whether 'imagined' or not, they have proven important and wise. And my guides have continued to change over time. My first guide, or Power Animal was a Turtle. I was slightly embarrassed to admit that my power animal was such a lethargic, cold-blooded, and slow-moving creature. However, over time I have also learned that there is medicine in anything that serves to share an energy with me.

What I mean by this, is that in Nature, which is very special to me, I can find 'medicine' in many things. For example, I find calming energy in the rustle of Aspen leaves. I find gentle and patient perseverance and strength in Ponderosa Pines. I find Motherly protective energy in the mama bears that roam the woods where I live every summer, and I find grounding energy in the smell of rich soils in my garden.

In the Turtle, I learned the medicine to be symbolic of:

- Ability to stay grounded, even in moments of disturbances and chaos
- Slowing down, pacing yourself
- Determination, persistence
- Emotional strength and understanding
- Ancient wisdom
- The world, of the Earth

Anything that teaches, heals, or stimulates an energy within me is called 'sacred medicine'. And, it is always available when I call.

Was my Turtle some external spiritual entity? Was my Turtle some imagery from my subconscious? Well, I have to submit, that I don't know. But, what I do know, is that I learned groundedness, patience, and began my journey towards emotional understanding from my studies into Native American Animal Medicine around the Turtle. And, these were to prove invaluable to me as I ventured ever and ever closer to the Gate of Hell. So, I would turn the question around and ask, "Does it matter, if it provides Medicine either way?"

So, Turtle was another Virgil to me in the early days.

My journey began with these types of Shamanic and Indigenous practices. I've been blessed to be able to explore this lifestyle and tradition deeply since. And, my pilgrimage was going to take many different paths as I made my way deeper.

And although each tradition I encountered felt so very uniquely different from others, I found that they were all speaking to me the same message, simply in diverse tongues.

They were, and are. all connected by….. The Golden Thread.

The Golden Thread

"Begin to weave and the Divine will provide the Thread"
                                                    Author unknown

Real-life 'Virgils' are all around us. They show up as counselors, self-help books, healing communities, gurus, priests, spirit or power animals, rituals, and so on. Many will not be seen as they are, until you look back years from now. But, appear they most assuredly do.

Some that have crossed my path have been:
- 12 Step Programs
- Yogic/Tantric Teachers
- Native American & Shamanic Traditions
- Tao / Zen Masters
- Counselors
- Women's Empowerment Circles
- Energetic Practitioners
- Meditation Practices
- Jungian Psychology and Bill Campbell's writings
- Shadow Work
- Ecstatic Prayer Dance Communities
- Multitudes of Authors
- And so on, and so on….

There are certain tenets that I have found common amongst all of these varied methodologies, and I call this the Golden Thread. For me, the Golden Thread has been another Virgil, my guide. This 'thread' has been my compass to align with those people and practices that I relate to and trust as integral for me. And, I've found the same thread of tenets in nearly every major theology, tradition, and philosophy.

They all lay out a path something like this:
1. Surrender leads to...
2. Introspection, which leads to...
3. Transformation, which leads to....
4. Embracing, owning, wisdom, and giving back to others.

The traditional 12-Step Program can be broken out, each successive 3 steps at a time, in the same way (I've included them for you as an Appendix), as does the Indigenous Medicine Wheels around the world. One aspect of the Medicine Wheel looks like this- starting in the East moving clockwise:

The Golden Thread unbeknownst to me early on, taught me a valuable lesson and one that is the very premise of success when finding my way through the Dark Forest. That is,
"I am solely responsible for EVERYTHING that happens in my life."

Let's be clear here, that does not mean that you are responsible for every circumstance you have in your life. What it does mean, is that you have the ultimate responsibility for how you show up 'to' the circumstances of your life. And, this is non-negotiable.

There are thousands of other 'maps' to this type of personal journey. And, I would submit, that there are vastly more similarities than there are differences between them, like the 12-Step Program and the Medicine Wheel have. I would recommend a healthy dose of curiosity as any new map crosses your path during your journey.

And, along with these maps that are tied together with the Golden Thread, let me introduce you to…. the Big Virgil.

The Power of Evolution

Although you may not have a belief system that includes Evolution as a tangible force that supports your expedition, one taken without this as a given, is one that will include more struggle and force. You'll be missing out on a powerful energy whose prime directive is to help guide you through your excursion, to a successful reunion with your Beatrice.

At this point, I hope you've surrendered to the mystery that lies ahead, and you need to know that you are more than you think you are. And more importantly, something, somewhere, wants you to make this journey.

There is a Universal intelligence that lies at the quantum level of all things, and it ebbs and flows with an unconditional desire to Evolve.

As Barbara Marx Hubbard explains it,

"Evolution is the expression of universal intelligence, now becoming conscious of itself within us, as us."

Once that door is open and you've revealed your willingness to surrender your attachments to the *'shoulds'*, the *'coulds'*, the what *"ifs'*, hang on tight because you've entered into the natural flow of all things which is toward Evolution. It's an inescapable current.

Evolution is undeniable, therefore, trustworthy. All one needs to do is to take a walk outside to know this to be true. If you take a close look at something in nature, a flower or tree, a stream or snowflake, a neighbor's dog or a playground of children, and allow the wonder of its journey to enter into your awareness, how can evolution not be a constant that is part of you too?

Take for example, a flower. Look at it, smell it, touch it. Consider the many extraordinary paths it has had, just to be here, right now, being held in your hand as you experience it.

It has a genetic code that determines its shape, and each code has undergone timeless change to be here as it is now. Each petal is a compilation of elements that were created billions of years ago now constructed elementally as it now. And, each element, particle and energy alike, will move into its next form in its future, over and over again, each time in form slightly different and evolved from its current. It is constantly in a state of becoming, something else, something more evolved to survive its evolving environment.

Evolution is a constant of our Universe, it is a primary goal at the quantum and energetic level of every living and non-living thing. Why not participate?

With evolution in mind, we can fathom the idea of co-creation when we become a conscious participant in our own individual evolution. Accepting this realization becomes a powerful implement to wield, a really big tool in our toolbox.

And, the really amazing thing is that even if we don't choose to acknowledge or co-partner with universal evolution, the Universe participates anyhow, with or without us! So, when we partake in the undeniable, we can consciously step into the flow and become a valuable co-creator with Evolution, of a better future for ourselves.

We can thus accelerate the natural process by being in alignment with natural intelligence which exists for this purpose. Surrender to the inevitable and support what the Universe wants, your personal evolution. It is going to be a Virgil for you. Even if you don't acknowledge it, it is always there, regardless of your awareness or participation.

Somehow Dante knew this I believe. As he is about to begin his journey with Virgil, he looks to the Heavens, understanding that the Universe is also engaged in his exploit, and petitions the Divine.

Dante exclaims, *"O Muses, O high genius, now assist me!"*

Vestibule of Hell

As Dante is led by Virgil through the Forest, and they approach the Gate hidden deep in the growing darkness, Dante sees the words inscribed above the entrance.

"All hope abandon, ye who enter in!"

These words in somber colour I beheld
Written upon the summit of a gate;
Whence I: "Their sense is, Master, hard to me!"

And he to me, as one experienced:
"Here all suspicion needs must be abandoned,
All cowardice must needs be here extinct.
Dante's Inferno Canto III

Dante hears the anguished screams of the 'Uncommitted' as he enters the Vestibule. At this stage of the Inferno, the souls reside here who took no sides in life, neither for good or evil, but were merely concerned with themselves.

Through the Gates they stride, into the entrance of another world. Within and around the Vestibule, Dante meets the first of many 'Shades,' or lost souls. Between the world behind the Vestibule and those worlds afterward, stalled between entrance and exit, are the souls that 'took no sides' but their own. Punishment at this level is simply that of being a part of neither world. And as Dante will soon discover, at each descending landscape, or Circle as they are called, he will find the souls in ever-increasing depths of sin. In each succeeding realm, the punishments invariably fit the crime and grow in intensity and gruesomeness.

And, our inner work here will continue to excavate at ever-deepening levels, with intensity as we progress as well.

If we were to dive straight to the bottom, we would most probably not have a foundation from which to understand what we would find when we got there. The landscape would be so foreign that compassion wouldn't be present and certainly the acceptance that comes with presence wouldn't yet be in our arsenal. It is a process of Evolution, one Circle at a time.

And, there would be so much missed along the way.

In Dante's experience as he progresses downward, it is very interesting how he reacts and it is a clue to our own work. He starts at the Vestibule, willing to meet the Uncommitted with empathy, understanding, and sympathy. As he progresses, his sympathy dissolves and eventually turns to righteous indignation. But, this is yet to come.

I relate to this passage through the Vestibule, because I started with a thinking that yes, I have these minor faults, but everyone has them, so they weren't so bad. I can forgive others for their faults with an empathy equal to Dante's, once I owned that I had them too. This thinking, at first, allowed me to justify deeds of my own doing. And, I took no sides.

As with the souls stuck between Heaven and Hell in the Vestibule who are not allowed entrance anywhere, I used empathy as a tool to vindicate my minor infractions, like selfishness. It is when this seemingly human, therefore forgivable, frailty grows from this place of misguided forgiveness, that harm is eventually done to ourselves and inflicted upon the others in our lives. It grows in severity and gruesomeness.

As Dante looks closer at the Uncommitted, he notices that the naked and futile souls are racing around in the mist in eternal pursuit of elusive blank banners. As they relentlessly chase the banners which symbolize the meaninglessness of their activity on Earth, they are chased by swarms of wasps and hornets who sting them into action. At their feet lie maggots and worms which drink the putrid mixture of blood, pus, and tears that flow down their bodies from the hornet stings.

The futile chase for the blank banner is similar to ours when we wander through the pre-scripted design of life. It is the state from which we came, from our Valley of Desolation, our blindness to our own individuation. The Uncommitted are analogous to our not committing, but heedlessly and meaninglessly existing.

The surface expression of this meaninglessness is where we turn our attention to first.

Our lives are meaningful, regardless of how we choose to live them. Some may have more bells and whistles or be visible to more people than others. But, they are all meaningful, when we choose to live by meaning. Meaning, means with conscious intention.

What gets in our way of living intentionally, are the layers and layers of belief systems we have collected along the way. As a human, we have need to organize our thoughts and the world around us, in fact, neurologically our brains are designed to do this. We do this in so many ways.

We collect our experiences, cultural values, familial standards, religious principals, and so on. And, we call this "me."

This identity of "me" is based on this conglomerate of belief systems. A belief is something that I "think" is true based on my collection of experiences confirming or denying those beliefs. And, these beliefs become so strongly ingrained after years of shoring up, that they become prison walls.

These belief systems need to be deconstructed. And the beauty of the practices, is that the simple realization that you've been chasing a blank banner (or a false belief) is that this is usually enough to produce an epiphany. The epiphany that you are not Uncommitted, that you are in fact, Committed to living by your own Truth.

Hornets and Wasps

I like this analogy because the first round of belief deconstruction stings a bit. It's those beliefs that we don't even recognize that we have. And know this, the deconstruction doesn't all happen at once. It is a lifetime practice. They will rise to the surface from this day forward once we unleash the openness and willingness to be curious about them.

There are levels of belief, but first, we'll take a look at the surface beliefs.

Belief Deconstruction Practice

You'll need a journal or pad of paper. I want you to write down a list of beliefs that you think you may have about everything you can:

Inner Beliefs:
What I believe about my:
- Self
- Body
- Career / Success
- Sex / Gender
- Attitudes
- Soul, spirit, or spiritual self
- God / Spirit / Source
- Family

- Abilities and limitations

Outer Beliefs:
What I believe about others and:
- Relationships
- Sexual Orientation
- Handicaps, illnesses
- Family
- Government
- World
- Good and Evil
- Skin Color
- Truth
- Church

Next, select the chosen few that have an emotional charge attached to them. This means they feel 'strong' to you, that they are more than just an opinion and they elicit a stronger reaction within you. You don't need to dissect the feeling yet, just recognize that you simply have it and circle them.

Examine each in turn and ask:
1. Can I be sure that it's true? And if so, how?
2. Has this belief served me in a 'good' way or 'bad' way in my life so far?
3. Who or when did I learn this belief from?
4. Why did I choose to believe it?
5. What did I avoid by having this belief?
6. How have I used this belief?
7. Have I ever seen this belief not be true? How often?
8. If I didn't have this belief, would I be different, or behave differently?

Let me offer an example from my own Belief Deconstruction.

Belief: I believe that men are all letches.

Examination:
1. I can be sure, because most of them I meet sooner or later act like a letch.
2. This belief has served me in keeping me distant from letches.
3. I believe I learned this as a young girl when the boys tried to sexually molest me behind the school.
4. I choose to keep believing because it kept happening.
5. By staying away, I avoided being abused.
6. I've used this belief to stay safe.
7. Well actually, not 100% of the time.
8. If I didn't believe this, I might be more open to giving each man a chance to be different.

Next, let's examine the underlying emotions. Ask yourself the following:

1. When I think of where this belief came from, how do I feel? How strongly? Really feel into this and allow your emotion/feeling to grow.
2. Where does this feeling live in my body? What shape, color, tone, texture does it have?
3. Breathe into that part of your body, and keep breathing until you feel it release, relax, and flow.

In my example, I explored the tension I held in my belly. I encouraged it to grow, and I could hear the boys behind the school laughing at me. At first, I felt fear about them trying to push me up against the wall and I couldn't stop them. Then, I heard them laughing and this elicited a very strong emotion of anger, rage, and shame.

I then detached from the story, and isolated the emotion of anger and shame and felt deeply into that. As I allowed this emotional charge it's space, just the emotion alone without the 'story', it began to feel more like sadness. And, it kept flowing....into something else.

The final questions are ones that need a lot more reflection time.

- Is this still true for you?
- If it's not, how do you believe now?

I sat with this reflection for a long time, allowing it time to ebb and flow, and eventually settle. I came to a discharged truth. I found that yes, I still believe that some men can behave like letches, and that behavior is wrong. Some women behave like letches too. But projecting this onto all men, has not served me well. I have been distant in relationships and as I will share later, this ended up manifesting into very unhealthy sexual behaviors of my own.

However, I found that I must still be discerning and still be cautious if someone indicates that they might behave badly in a sexual way toward me and create the distance necessary to protect myself.

And, more importantly, I learned that the laughter I heard was what was triggering my deeper emotional response. It was what was under the surface of my belief, fueling it. I also had some shame issues that were driving my belief that kept me safe in projecting that all men were letches. We will do a deeper dive into emotional wounding later on, but first let's settle for simply identifying beliefs.

For me, this means at this point I knew a few things:

1. I had been projecting onto all men this sense of fear and not being safe which kept me at a safe distance.
2. My anger towards men was misplaced, because not every man acts that way.
3. I have some shame hiding deeper inside that I will need to look at someday. And, maybe I was creating this anger and judgment in order to not look at the shame?
4. At the time of this belief's creation, it was a valid and understandable response to an unfortunate circumstance. It was created to keep a young, naïve girl safe.

I've used this personal experience to highlight something about beliefs. We can create them for many reasons, and the least of which is that they are true. The ones that are charged are, by and large, something important for us to pay attention to.

Beliefs cause us to create false messaging about ourselves and judgments towards others. When simple beliefs have emotional charges attached, they are harder to get under, but much more powerful and important to dig into. They are the ones that cause us suffering, and manifest themselves in behavior.

If you find it hard to excavate your listing of beliefs, start with when you have behaved poorly. This will be an indicator that something you judged about a situation or person that was created from a belief, is the culprit.

Maggots and Worms

In Dante's gruesome telling, he mentions the maggots and worms that feed from the wounds of the Uncommitted. We too, have those types of beliefs. We just need to dig a little deeper to get to those. These are our core beliefs, those that are even more difficult to identify.

This can be because the surface belief is really 'linked' to many others like a chain. And, they burrow deeply into our psyche and feed off of inborn natures, repressed emotions, memories, and wounds. And they fester until we break a link in the chain.

The most effective link to break of course, is the original one, the one at the bottom of the pit. This one may take years to fully dig out like a bad splinter. In the meantime, breaking any link in the chain can be helpful as we begin, and the more we continue to practice being conscious to our charges, or triggers, the closer we will continue to get to the bottom. Trust in the process, and keep vigilant. And, more than anything, be compassionate with yourself as you start to unearth the inner maggots.

In your Belief Listing you made, you will dismantle some beliefs only to find they are linked to others, again a chain of beliefs. If that is the case, keep going until you can go no deeper. As I did with Shame, I kept this on my list of 'work still to be done' as I couldn't find my answer to why I believed I was shameful initially. As I continued into the Inferno, I would deal with this later but it simply wasn't time yet for me to understand it. This is exactly why Dante had to take one step at a time, because meeting the Devil all at once, is deadly.

Accept that some of this work is an unfolding. It will unfold, once you have reached the depth that it lives in and not before. This is the Universe's way of keeping us from going straight to the bottom Circle of Hell, and it is designed to preserve some level of our sanity while we descend.

Back to beliefs....Our deeper core beliefs lie under the surface of our conscious thought, which is where most of our originating thoughts come from. Freud described our mind in three levels and used an iceberg as an analogy. The conscious thought was the 10% of the iceberg above the water's surface. The 90% under the surface was our sub-conscious, then our unconscious.

We can liken our journey down thus far, as reaching the waterline of that iceberg. We are now leaving the Vestibule, and headed to our first Circle of the Inferno.

Let me lay out a bit of a roadmap, so that you can keep this in mind as we progress ever downward. In Dante's Inferno, the Vestibule is only the entrance to the Circles of Hell. Not to discourage you, but we have a long journey ahead.

There are a total of nine Circles. The first few Circles after leaving the Vestibule are reflective of our perpetuating the 'harm' done. The first 3 Circles are collectively called the Circles of Indulged Passion, meaning they are the remnants of having lived blindly, absorbed within the design of the Valley of Oblivion. We really haven't caused any harm per se, since we lived amongst those that too, were in the same Valley. But living accordingly has left us with damage that we must shine a light on in order to acknowledge and possible repair before moving underneath into the realm of who we are.

It is the power of inner relation, that ability to build a new relationship with our inner landscape, that propels us and creates our foundation. Our foundation for building a better life starts with unraveling the foundation of our past.

The 4-6th Circles are symbolic of the Inner Harms we do to ourselves. Of course, all of the Circles do inner harm, but we will dig underneath and see how our Outer World is a pure projection of our Inner World and false reality, thus denying us our true vision.

The final Circles, 7-9, are archetypically those harms of the preceding Circles, but where we have acted on them with our behavior. It is the Outer Harms that we have enacted in our lives, culminating in the final 9th Circle, where Satan is held in bondage. We need to come to terms with how we've behaved, so as to not continue to harm, condemning ourselves to eternal damnation.

One Circle at a time....

As I progressed through my excavation, each step took me deeper and deeper in the depths of my own psyche, reaching for the day where I'd find myself 'clear.' However, know that day will never come for you or I, and be joyful about it.
For it is not the answer to the question, "Who am I and why am I the way I am," that is the final destination. It is the power within the mere asking, as each questioning reaches new depths that turns out to be the Eden at the journey's end.

The question might become, "How are these life experiences here to help me evolve and move forward?"

And lo! towards us coming in a boat
An old man, hoary with the hair of eld,
Crying: "Woe unto you, ye souls depraved!
          Dante's Inferno Canto III

And, lo! toward us in a bark
Comes on an old man, hoary white with eld,
Crying, "Woe to you, wicked spirits!"
Canto III., lines 76–78.

    Virgil has taken Dante to the river Acheron, and the ferryman, Charon, approaches to take them across. During their crossing, Dante faints and awakens on the other side, and his journey into the Divine terrain begins.

Upper Hell: Circles of Indulged Passion

The first few Circles embody the most minor of our inner transgressions, those that the first Beast, the She-Wolf of Wantoness symbolized. This is the home of the lustful, gluttonous, hoarders, and wasters, greedy, and wrathful. This is the landscape of the abuses we do within ourselves to ourselves. We have abused our human faculty of reason, our mind, and allowed it to control us with apathy, blindness, and fear. We have allowed unfettered passions to be indulged.

Here, we are exploring the mire we create when we believe we are in control, when think we control our lives, and believe we can control everyone and everything around us. We use control to manage our lives, within the idea that we are the center of our Universe.

In the 12-Step Program, the very first step is:

We admitted we were powerless over _____ and that our lives had become unmanageable.

It's a great place to start, by simply admitting we aren't in control....of anything. We aren't in control of anything other than how we choose to live, consciously, given the circumstances we are presented with.

When I got sober and read the First Step, I realized that this step is actually two steps combined. But until they converged in my Valley of Oblivion, I hadn't reached a point where I was in enough pain to be willing to change. That is human nature.

Until the pain of the present becomes stronger than our fear of the future, we do not make change.

Let me explain this convergence of the two parts of Step One a bit further. I could have made the statement that I was powerless over my drinking probably, if I'm honest, since I was in high school. However, I hadn't failed the second test, that of manageability of my life, until I was 43 years old. I was what was called a functional drunk. I could drink and effectively hide it well enough so that my life hadn't fallen completely apart. Until I couldn't....and it did.

I was functional at work and at home for the most part. I had learned well the value of lying and 'fixing' things so that I could continue to drink. I was also what we call, a black-out drunk where, for the last 6 years of my drinking chapter, I would wake up the following morning not remembering having gone to bed the night before.

With the creativity born out of desperation, I learned early on in those six years to stash a journal of the night's events so that I could read it the next morning and not make any mistakes that might give my secret away. You see, while in a blackout, you are conscious-just not recording anything into memory for the following day. So, I starting noting down arguments and my position during them, conversations, events, movie names, and so on. The problem was that I kept forgetting where I put my journal. Funny now, but at the time, it was a critical strategy to my overall functionality-illusion.

Regardless of what malady you place into the blank line in Step One above, the meaning is the same. And for those who consider themselves not addicted to something- sex, work, food, drama, etc.- I might argue you could insert MY SELF there, to begin with. Because that is where we find ourselves at this stage of our epic travail; we are powerless over how we think, behave, and choose. We are still connected to too many of the implanted hooks, those that are impaling the proverbial worms that dangle in the water to grab our attention and keep us connected to the delusion.

I love the paradoxes that present themselves as you make your way along. They can become valuable and fun food for thought. For example, by surrendering to your powerlessness, you begin to regain your power. The Tao is a favorite philosophy of mine, where paradox is a unique way to explain the obvious and the non-obvious.

When I let go of who I am, I become what I might be. Interestingly, this speaks to our surrender of everything we thought to be true when living in the Valley of Desolation, according to the lie of the design. It also speaks to letting go of the idea that we can 'control' anything, and by accepting the fact that we do not control anything, we become….It might also speak to the possibility of what is real, when I 'disconnect' from the hooks, the worms, the line.

Yet another paradox for us to practice and play with, is that *by going into our inner spaces, we connect to our outer spaces.* Let's venture there a bit….

Circle of Limbo

For such defects, and not for other guilt,
Lost are we and are only so far punished,
That without hope we live on in desire.
Dante's Inferno Canto IV

When Dante awakens, he finds that he has crossed the River Acheron and Virgil leads him to the first Circle of the abyss, The Circle of Limbo. The souls encountered here are those who chose to not accept salvation and in early Christian doctrine this would relate to not being baptized. They had lived their lives choosing human virtue over spiritual virtue. In giving up any desire to explore beyond human reason, they lived without hope.

This is all to say, they centered their thoughts solely on themselves and their logical reasoning, and in doing so, forsook the opportunity to believe in anything greater than themselves.

Their punishment was that they would live throughout eternity, feeling insatiable desire, knowing no hope of quenching their cravings.

This is also the basis of the 12-Step Program's 2nd Step. We came to believe in a power greater than ourselves to restore us to sanity.

We have visited the ideas already of plugging into the Evolutionary Process of the Universe, as well as inviting guides and greater wisdom sources to accompany us. Now we'll take a look at actually experiencing this higher power.

What is the greatest obstacle to this? It is our mind and its insatiable stream of thoughts. The philosopher Descartes stated that, "I think, therefore I am." This I find in grave error, because he equated thinking with Being and our identity with thinking. We live in a world that is always moving and we are constantly in a state of needing to think. There is very little appreciation for the state of non-thinking.

Thinking is nearing the point of disease in our societies. And we think we are using our minds, but in reality, it is the other way around. Our minds use us.

We've allowed them, our human minds, to rule, and have lost touch with being a Human Being. Embracing this, one can become what Eckert Tolle calls the 'Watcher.' We can 'watch the thinker' and he states, "You then begin to realize that there is a vast realm of intelligence beyond thought, that thought is only a tiny aspect of. You also realize that all the things that truly matter- beauty, love, creativity, joy, inner peace- arise from beyond the mind. You begin to awaken."

So you may be asking then, am I saying that our higher self, or that 'something' that is greater than ourselves, is within us? I would have to say that I won't answer this. I would rather you experience this yourself, and define what 'it' is for yourself. I am saying that the definition of 'something greater' is for each one of us to come to our own understanding of. And, I am saying that this is a critical stepping stone in our pilgrimage to find this understanding for ourselves.

I have referred to the Golden Thread previously, and this is another essential tenet of any personal growth practice. Early in every method, I have found that some type of recognition of acknowledgement of spirituality is a necessity. Let me be clear here however, that spirituality differs greatly from traditional religious doctrine in that spirituality used in these approaches is not bound by any rules, requirements, or dogma. Spirituality here represents the complete openness to the interpretation of your own choosing, as long as it is something greater than ourselves. That's it.

In exploring what this is for you, I invite you to the practice of The Watcher, which is an invitation to delve into a new dimension of consciousness and discover something, maybe Divine even.

Note, as this is our first Meditation Practice, I will be offering an initial induction and relaxation practice here. For the remainder of any meditation practices, I will be referring back to this Meditation Induction Practice as the first step for all of them. It is an essential step to any Meditation, that you start off with a lengthy and slow descent below your conscious level of thinking. As in Shamanic Journeying, we are wanting to induce a Theta brain wave, which allows us to access deeper levels of consciousness but not fall asleep.

Please feel free to utilize any method you prefer to begin the Meditations with, in place of this if you wish. I have also provided this and all Meditations in the DVD that is available as well, for your convenience. If you choose, I also highly recommend that you record yourself, reading these Meditations, and guide yourself through them.

The Watcher Practice:

Meditation Induction:
- *Relax, and breathe…(repeat this a few times over 3 minutes, yes, 3 minutes at a minimum).*
- *Bring your awareness to the top of your head, and feel every cell. (going very slowly…) now your face…… ears……. nose….. neck……. shoulders……., make your way down the rest of your body. Take your time…..Feel every cell as you go, holding each in your growing awareness as you move farther downward.*
- *Bring your breath to any part that is difficult to move through….breathe your awareness 'through' any density that you come across.*
- *Feel each cell come alive as you bring your awareness to them. Feel them sparkle, or buzz, or?*
- *Breathe….*
- *After you've reached the tips of every toe, repeat this rinse and enliven each cell even more. (Repeat the above at least 1 more time, take your time with this, it's critically important to enliven your connection to your body first).*
- *Breathe….(throw this in every so often as breathing moves energy)*
- *That's good, feel your whole body tingle with aliveness. Bring your entire physical body into your awareness field……*
- *Now, expand your awareness to the energy field that flows through each cell, that flows through your body.*
- *Moving your way out now, feel your energy as it surrounds your body…. Feel your energy merge with the flow of all energy….the evolutionary energy of the Universe….*

The Watcher Meditation:
- Bring your attention now to your thoughts as they pass through your mind. Let them pass like clouds in the sky.
- Pick one....one random thought. Be curious about where it came from....how did it arrive here, what thought preceded it, and what thought preceded that...continue following the chain of thoughts to its lowest level that you can.....simply with curiosity.
- Now....release it. Feel the gap of no-mind between the thoughts.
- As the thoughts begin to stream again, pull back your attention, and become the Watcher....of your thoughts.
- Ask yourself, if I am watching these random thought patterns, who am I? Who is the Watcher? (explore this for as long as you wish)
- As the Watcher, turn your attention to the present moment. Become intensely aware of you, the Watcher experiencing this moment. (stay here as long as you wish)
- When you are ready, bring your attention back to your breathing, and begin to gently move your fingers and toes.
- Awaken as you choose.
- Journal your experience if you wish.

Although you can read through this in just a minute or so, extend it to 20 minutes with lots of space for your immersion and complete curiosity.

The intention of this practice is three-fold.
- First, it is to experience for yourself, that you are not your thoughts.

- Secondly, there is a presence inside us that is more than our physical expression. There is a deeper self who is capable of bringing mindfulness into the moment.
- And lastly, it is to take you beyond what you previously thought of as your 'self' and that the presence you cultivate is inconceivably greater than what you think you are.

I recommend doing this simple meditation practice as often as you can. As with anything we do, we get better with practice. You can then take this practice with you, into moments of real life, while walking, while making dinner, while making love. Bring this presence with you into your life, and watch how the world responds to you from your centering of your presence.

This may be the single most important step of any of them, because with full presence anything in our lives can be navigated by accessing resources that the Universe, God, Buddha, Creator, pure consciousness has made available to us. You have invited something unknown, <u>something greater into your realm of awareness</u>.

Is this inner realm really a manifestation of an outer realm within us? Is this level of deeper consciousness just part of our sub-conscious brain or is it a connection to something Divine- or are they the same thing? Is the Watcher me, or God?

Well, I might answer, does it matter?

What we do know now, is that there lies within us the portal to something greater than our logical reasoning self, a something that is greater than the "I" as I know it.

With that tool in our belt, we are ready to explore the next level. Virgil, lead on……

Circle of Lust

As Dante approaches the second Circle of Hell proper, he meets the serpentine Minos, who judges each condemned soul by wrapping his tail around his/her body so many times, to signify the number of the Circle, to which the soul is condemned. After Virgil convinces Minos to allow an undead soul to enter, which is of course, not the norm in Hell, Dante passes through into the Circle of Lust.

Dante and Virgil enter into a 'place where no thing gleams,' where torrential rains fall ceaselessly and winds tear through the air. The souls are swept helplessly, to and fro, through the eternal storm, damned to never rest. Virgil explains that these carnal malefactors are condemned for allowing their appetites, or unquenchable lust, to sway their reason.

It hither, thither, downward, upward, drives them;
No hope doth comfort them for evermore,
Not of repose, but even of lesser pain.

"The first of those, of whom intelligence
Thou fain wouldst have," then said he unto me,
"The empress was of many languages.

To sensual vices she was so abandoned,
That lustful she made licit in her law,
To remove the blame to which she had been led.
Dante's Inferno, Canto V

In my journey, it was not a linear path like Dante's, I was blown 'to and fro' relentlessly. I wandered between practices learning many of the pieces that today, I can somewhat retrospectively piece together in a more logical path. However, I think the value in wandering comes from the continued revisiting of each 'step' over and over again, as was needed in my life. And, revisiting this particular Circle is one of my favorite wanderings.

Virgil has led Dante to a Circle that lies just under our thought patterns, into a deeper realm of desire, where these souls had no control over theirs during their lifetime. They were blown around by their unfettered appetites.

Desire is found between the worlds of reason and emotion. And, when we begin to deal with our emotions, our wandering <u>truly</u> begins, as this is a realm where nothing is linear. We begin to add emotion into our growth and healing, building towards emotional intelligence. From this point forward, our emotions are an integral piece of every succeeding step of our journey.

Desire is not a bad thing. At its root is your emotion of love that wishes to have more of the love-inducing tangible or intangible thing. We desire what makes us feel good and what we love. And feeling is the in-body manifestation of an emotion. Pure emotion however, is simply a flowing field of energy.

But we can create a self-destructive cycle when a thought pattern triggers an emotion, which then feeds the thought pattern which feeds even more emotion, and on and on it goes. When the thought pattern is not necessarily a healthy one, we can endlessly be blown around.

Recognize however, we're missing an integral piece of the picture here. Since 90% of our thinking is below the waterline of conscious thought, this means that most of our emotion is stirred by the depths and currents of our sub-conscious thought. In fact, emotions, being a flow of energy, are also being generated from outside of our mind. Energy is what everything is, material and non-material alike, at the quantum level. So this translates to a lot of energy flowing in and around us that isn't within the bounds of 'my ownership,' per se. Going further, where does my energy, that which is mine end, and yours begin?

For now, we simply want to stop being blown about by unfettered desire, at the mercy of the energies that blow in and from the depths, and toss us around relentlessly. We want to become intimate with and a partner to our emotions. And if a large part of our emotional state comes from someplace beneath our conscious thought (which we are more than), then can the emotions be guideposts, or even hidden portals to that which lies under the surface? Of course, they must.

There are many reasons to cultivate a connection to our emotions. The flowing fields of emotional energies are like Dante's *'empress of many languages'* which I believe to be an inference to a woman's vast flow of wild emotions.

They can enhance our lives with many essences, dimensions, and expressions. But, like the shades of this Circle, we can fall prey to vice without blame when we give our emotions a throne they don't deserve or believe that we are at their mercy with no control panel.

The result is that when we are not connected and fully present, they will still manifest and they end up feeding physical and mental illness. Also, just as with thoughts, we need to discover that we are not our emotions. There are times in our lives that we feel they are a life sentence and we feel as though they command, and we obey. However, they need to be dethroned as Master, and rather, knighted as Divine Messenger.

For it is the ability to be *consciously with* emotion, again being a Watcher, that we can build this new relationship. But even more than Watcher, we will find as we odeeper in our journey, that there is much to be learned by becoming very intimate, in fact a Lover to, and in relationship with our emotions.

First, because emotions can be quite foreign and frightening, we need to break free of the serpentine Minos within our psyche, that part of us that subjects us to condemnation when certain emotions are allowed to sit on their throne and rule us. They can become internal and external tempests, blowing us helplessly to and fro. And when they do, without a doubt given our desire to be all things happy and pain-free, we are likely to be subject to the appetites of the winds blowing around us always.

Simple Emotional Awareness Practice

You can do this at anytime, anywhere, around anyone. And, I recommend you do this often each day.

Close your eyes (you will get so good at this, that you won't need this step, but it helps you dive deeper and practice at first).

Looking without your eyes, bring your awareness to the inside of your body. Ask yourself, "What am I feeling?"

That's it....

Don't analyze. Just stay aware and present to what is inside. Feel the energy of the emotion. It may inevitably take a bit of practice for some, because we are, especially men, acculturated to not feel.

There's so much more to be said about emotion but, for now suffice it to say, that just getting in touch with them can be a huge step. Once you can gain some proficiency with simply connecting to them, acknowledging them, feeling them, you may recognize that they are in conflict with your mental chatter. This can seem confusing, but is in fact, a marvelous revelation.

This is because again, most of our emotional states arise from levels woven throughout unconscious thought. Thus, they are guideposts to what's going on deeper inside of us. Therefore, don't be fooled into thinking that they are out of touch with where we are now. In fact, they are more accurate indicators as to what's really going on inside us, more so than our conscious/surface-level thoughts.

With this in mind, they become portals into our sub-conscious. Portals are direct tunnels into our unknown, and we'll use them in the deeper Circles. They are a gateway and channel to our deepest selves. For now, simply open up to connecting with them and getting to know them. Just as with thought, we are not them, but they are a valuable ally in any case.

In doing so, you've taken the huge step of removing them from their insolent pedestal, and engaging with them as Mystical Messengers.

Once you can become proficient at actually discerning 'how you feel' and what emotional-energetic tide is running through you at any time, you can begin to be curious about the emotions that are your default. More importantly as you move deeper towards emotional intelligence, you will begin to discern those emotions that are not in your default settings. They certainly exist and run through us. But, you may find that they have become frozen somewhere deep inside, or that you fear their rising to the surface. For now, we will leave them safely where they are and focus on the tides that run freely.

When these Messengers arrive, they rarely come alone. Often, they are joined by more than one emotion at a time, and this can be very confusing. I'm sure you've felt the tidal waves of anger, fear, and sadness, all at the same time. Maybe this threesome is governed more by fear at times. Maybe at other times, the anger has more venom. Or, maybe they are even joined by something 'other' that is so tightly wound up that you can't clearly understand what it is. These can all be unraveled with presence and curiosity one thread at a time.

Or, they can be simply accepted for now, for the mix that they are. There are probably many tendrils of 'reason' that they have partnered up at this moment in your life. Unraveling these can take some skill and we will certainly get there. But, as with any new relationship, especially one as intimate as our emotions, we become empathetic to them and curious about who they and the messages they bring to begin with.

There are certainly those emotions too, that make us uncomfortable and that just don't feel 'good.' For right now, recognize them when they come. All we want to do when we start emotional excavating, is to find the willingness to share a few moments with them, and then let them pass. Get to know how they feel, the circumstances of when they like to visit, and how to let them go. Starting a relationship with our emotions starts in the body. Here is a short practice for this.

Emotional Landscaping

Start with the Meditation Induction Practice
- With your inner eye, look into your body, scan it, listen to it, feel into it.
- What is here for you now? What do you feel?
- Invite what you are feeling, to come nearer to the surface. Invite it to share itself with you, and you alone.
- When you find yourself feeling into the emotional mix that is within you in this moment, open up a blank canvas in your mind.
- Invite your emotional body to express itself onto your canvas, with color, texture, images, sounds- however it wants to express itself to you and you alone.
- Allow........ and watch (as your Watcher) with curiosity what the emotional landscape becomes for you.
- Allow yourself the curiosity and openness to this energetic landscape.
- When you're ready, thank your emotional body for sharing itself so creatively and intimately with you...and return to this fully present moment.

You may wish to journal about this, or if you are an artistic sort, try to capture this in a painting or song. Find some way to honor this sacred and secretly shared landscape.

And don't be surprised or judgmental about what shows up. Not all of the emotional landscapes will look like anything recognizable, or full of daisies and puppies. Although, some may....But, each is a gift.

The beauty of this practice is taking 'how' a feeling feels in the body, and allowing it to begin to express itself to you. There will come a time where we will give these emotions full permission to express themselves but some emotions and their partners need this coaxing technique. You also need to get to know them and recognize when they like to visit, simply as part of your inner landscape. You have started the very early building of a lifelong intimate relationship with those emotional energies that you will come to know as Mystic Messengers as we continue our trek.

Virgil leads Dante to the next Circle, a place of malodorous filth.

Circle of Gluttony

Huge hail, and water sombre-hued, and snow,
Athwart the tenebrous air pour down amain;
Noisome the earth is, that receiveth this.

Cerberus, monster cruel and uncouth,
With his three gullets like a dog is barking
Over the people that are there submerged.

Red eyes he has, and unctuous beard and black,
And belly large, and armed with claws his hands;
He rends the spirits, flays, and quarters them.
                            Dante's Inferno, Canto VI

Dante finds the next Circle similar to the last with an eternal storm drowning the landscape, but this time, it is a storm of filth, consisting of a vile, putrid slush that endlessly turns the Earth into a horrid, foul and freezing mire.

They meet the guardian at the gate, the three-headed worm-dog, Cerberus, who ravenously keeps the souls wallowing prostate in the freezing mire. He mauls and flays them with his claws as they howl like beaten dogs.

The souls or, as Dante calls them, the shadows in this domain are those who were Gluttonous in life. They had taken desire to the next level, to the extent that they voraciously avoided pain at any cost. Gluttony in Christianity is considered one of the seven carnal sins and manifests as excessive indulgence and grievous appetite or desire. It is the pursuit of pleasure over pain at any cost that has damned many a soul.

Thus, it is time my friend, to meet the Ego. As defined by Eckhart Tolle, best-selling author of *The Power of Now*, "Ego is the unobserved mind that runs your life when you are not present as the witnessing consciousness, the Watcher."

There's been much written over the last few decades about ego. And, most teachings are that our ego is evil and must be gotten rid of at any cost. However, I respectfully disagree.

Who can blame these poor tormented souls in the Circle of Gluttony? We all want to avoid pain in our lives. Our mind evolved very early on a mechanism to help us do just that.

Picture 10,000 years ago, living in a cave and needing to brave the elements and your existence as part of the food-chain. Tribal consciousness developed in order to survive, because living alone was a certain death sentence. Living with the tribe was not a right, it was a privilege and one needed to 'belong' in order to not be outcast and die.

Just as we did then, we do now. We must fit in and belong. This is also part of our Divine Nature, as we are a relational species, like it or not. This is elemental to our mere survival instinct. Thus, we created a part of us that desired above all else, to protect us from exile, which was the ultimate pain. This, is the sole function of the ego.

Therefore, the ego has a very important role. In fact, it deems itself to be life-sustaining and the protector against exile and death. Given this majestic role, it can't be deemed worthless or bad. And, it has done everything in its power to fulfill its duties, from our very first breath, and it has done a fantastic job.

When we were very young, at some point we felt threatened to be exiled. It may have been that day when we said something not quite right, or behaved badly in public. Likely, we've all heard our parent's scolding words, "Don't be a bad boy!", or "Stop that, you should be ashamed of yourself!" I posit that there isn't anything bad about our parents training us to fit into the tribe. However, our ego can take these types of interactions and, albeit innocently at first, create numerous protective defense mechanisms to ensure that we know how to belong 'properly.' These defense mechanisms create lots of drama as we grow and get lodged into our sub-conscious, affecting our conscious thoughts and emotions.

As my own expedition progressed over time, I had heard a lot about this ego. This ego sounded quite vile and diabolic, that I wanted nothing more than to separate myself from it. I looked for an easy way to understand my ego and how to deal with it. This is when I ran across Eckhart Tolle's books. He uses a concept called the 'pain-body'. This concept helped me carve away the harmful side of my ego and separate this from the more instinctual and basic objective of the ego.

Tolle describes it this way. *The pain-body is my term for the accumulation of old emotional pain that almost all people carry in their energy field. I see it as a semi-autonomous psychic entity. It consists of negative emotions that were not faced, accepted, and then let go in the moment they arose. These negative emotions leave a residue of emotional pain, which is stored in the cells of the body. There is also a collective human pain-body containing the pain suffered by countless human beings throughout history. The pain-body has a dormant stage and an active stage. Periodically it becomes activated, and when it does, it seeks more suffering to feed on. If you are not absolutely present, it takes over your mind and feeds on negative thinking as well as negative experiences such as drama in relationships. This is how it has been perpetuating itself throughout human history. Another way of describing the pain-body is this: the addiction to unhappiness.*

This description made a lot of sense to me. The antidote is basically the bringing of Presence when the pain-body becomes triggered, or activated. When we notice that the pain-body becomes triggered, we simply recognize this event for what it is. Recall that when we bring Presence, we enable ourselves to detach from the thoughts and emotions in the moment. They are not us, because we are the Watcher.

An interesting thing happens in that moment; the energy tied up in the pain-body transmutes. It changes into fuel for more Presence. Over time, and each time we do this, we are diffusing the power of the pain-body more and more. That doesn't mean it will go away completely someday, although this is a noble goal, but the hold it has on our lives becomes less and less strangling.

Cerberus, the 3-headed monster, can be imagined to be our pain-body, subjecting our lives to a storm of incessant fear, leaving us to wallow in the putrid quagmire of our drama.

And, as Tolle describes his antidote, it is more than just recognizing our pain-body and becoming fully present to it. It takes facing our pain-body, accepting it, then letting go of it in the moment. Since the pain-body is comprised of pain, I for one, didn't want to meet it.

Initially, I had also picked up much literature that was preaching processes similar to NLP, Neurolinguistic

Programming. They teach processes whereby one can reprogram, if you will, the inner language that we use within ourselves. It sounded perfect for me at the time. I spent lots of time on repositioning negative thought patterns into positive thought patterns. Think a happy thought...think a happy thought...think a happy thought.

And, I would feel good... until I didn't.

Although NLP may work for some, it simply didn't for me. There was an important missing component, which is the 'acceptance' piece. I had taken Tolle's steps, 1) Face negative thoughts or emotions, 2) Accept them, and 3) Let them go, and I'd forgotten step #2.

In retrospect, what I had fallen for was the easy way out. I wanted to effectively bypass my unhappiness. I had wanted to be present as I understood it then, and move right on past it to happiness. So what does it really mean to accept unhappiness?

Or worse yet, to accept pain?

Rumi said, *"The cure for the pain, is in the pain."*

During the latter half of my journey, I came across some powerful teachings that helped me understand wholeness and embodiment, which included teachings and practices with emotional embodiment. One of my most favorite teachers is Chameli Ardagh, who is the founder of Awakening Women. Most of my understandings of emotional relatedness and intelligence comes from this beloved guru.

Pain comes to us in many forms- loss, anxiety, fear, sadness, frustration, anger, hurt, shame, guilt, and so on. Most of these kinds of emotional energies lie very low in our vibrational field at a low frequency, although they are very strong. And our pain-body, as Tolle describes, is full of these.

Another way to think of pain, as Chameli teaches it, is to liken it to a frozen ice cube. Any emotion can become frozen within us, when not given the allowance to flow. When our ego decided it was too dangerous for us to feel some painful emotion, we locked it up, which froze it in place.

Thus, the more pain our ego shelters from our view, the greater the density of the pain-body. The only remedy lies in the thawing of the ice, the meeting of the pain, the release of the pain, one cube at a time.

The denser your pain-body, the longer this can take.

I used to do a lot of snowmobiling in Colorado, my home state. Avalanches are a frightening and dangerous part of that sport, especially when you venture into virgin valleys high in the Rockies. I learned caution and a high degree of respect for Mother Nature that way. I also learned that great big, deadly snow chunks start out as very fine, non-lethal powder at first. Momentum, gravity, and heat from friction freeze snow dust from the top, into masses of dense, frozen concrete chunks at the bottom.

Such is the life cycle of our pains. Regardless of how minute they may have begun, they have grown in density over time by being re-triggered numerous times. Now, that is not to say that our first experience with fear for example was insignificant or trivial. It is just to say, that they grow denser with time. Even parts of the avalanches I've seen, have started as a combination of powder and some very large chunks, all ending at the bottom differently than they began at the top.

Thus, unfreezing some of our fundamental pains may require applied heat over a lengthy time. Be patient and compassionate with yourself as you venture here. This isn't easy work to do, and, it's certainly not painless. However, one of the learnings from going deeply into pain, is that you do survive. Your ego is wrong, you don't perish and you will not die.

Survive, and then you'll find you're free to thrive.

Before we proceed, it would be negligent of me to not make a disclaimer here. This type of practice worked for me, because the pains that I had to release were not created from violence, other than that I created for myself. If you are someone who may have experienced severe abuse or trauma, I recommend working with a professional as you start to visit pain.

Most pain we will find will be birthed from experience we've had with others. Discern whether or not you're comfortable working alone or would benefit from working with someone else. But, do the work as bypassing isn't a viable option.

Take a deep breath, because we're about to start to free ourselves from the quagmire and filth.

This practice needs some preparation. Make sure you can carve out at least an hour or two to yourself. You want to make sure you aren't going to be disturbed and have plenty of alone space, and have some free space for a while afterward. And, you may want some Kleenex.

A note about Kleenex; don't reach for it too quickly.....don't steal this primal opportunity away from yourself. The key is to fully allow all of the vile, putrid, and filth to be released.

Also, certain types of pain are triggered and released differently. You have a lot of latitude with how you do this practice. If anger is the pain that you are working with for example, lower body movement and aggressive, muscular motion helps stir this emotion, and also helps this emotion to dissolve. However, sadness is more easily triggered by sitting and actually wallowing in it, and then releasing it ends best with gentleness...and Kleenex.

Bring whatever means you need to this practice in order to generate the emotion, to make it BIG, and allow for whatever you need to release it.

One final note before we begin. During this practice, allow an emotion to become another if that is what happens naturally to it. For example, under anger is typically sadness, shame or something much different than the surface anger. Allow for the flow, physically and emotionally. Trust that the surface emotion may be something different as you follow it, and flow with it. Trust...

Emotional Release and Flow Practice

1. Determine, without any reasoning, what pain is up for you in your life that you'd like to work with. Sometimes it is the one that you most fear. At first, select one that is lessor charged, just to get the hang of it.
2. Sit straight-backed and comfortably to start with. Do the Meditation Induction Practice.
3. Play some music that 'feels' like this emotion to you. Take special care to pick a piece that really brings you into the emotion you've chosen, which is reflective of how it FEELS. Try to find an instrumental piece without words.
4. Now, invite the emotion into your body and FEEEEEELLLL....
5. Feel the emotion, and if necessary, bring in the 'story' that makes it BIG. Relive it, over and over again, until you FEEEEELLLL.....
6. Now, release the story if you have connected to it, and simply make the raw emotion even BIGGER...(If stillness is needed, do it, if tribal dance is needed, do that, if screaming is needed, do that...do what you feel - the key is to make the emotion BIGGER than you think it is, take your foot off the brake and hit the accelerator as hard as you can)
7. With presence, where does this emotion live in your body? Can you locate it and describe it?
8. With curiosity, follow the emotion.....can you bring to mind earlier and earlier times when you've experienced this same feeling?

9. Follow and feel for as long as you can...stay in the fire of this emotion (the longer you can stay with it, the more thawing you'll get).
10. As you follow the emotion, your body will know what to do, just follow the impulse to cry, scream, wail, laugh - whatever expression you need to stay in this fire of the movement of your emotions. Let go fully, and allow.
11. When you've depleted this emotion as much as you can, become still and become aware of your body, and BREATHE into this part of your body where the emotion is right now.
12. Breathe, and let the emotion FLOW...into where ever it goes. If it takes you into a new realm of emotion, repeat the practice with the new emotion, making it big, and then becoming still with it, flowing. Until there are no more.
13. Relax, take some deep cleansing breaths for as long as is needed, and slowly, compassionately return as you feel ready.
14. Journal.

Once you've gone into the center of this pain and been willing to follow it to where ever it leads, fearlessly, and said, "I'm not afraid of you," you will know this emotion. You have created a new relationship with it. Congratulate yourself, for this is the work of the Hero and the Heroine. It is the work that shakes loose the inner emotional blocks, which can be some of the most challenging we will face.

And be gentle on yourself after any of this type of work. Heavy emotional practices will deplete you. When I do them, I notice what I call an Emotional Hangover. It can make me feel depressed, lethargic, and generally down for a time. Allow this too, for there is a place for rest in emotional recovery. Honor it, don't fight it or fall prey to self-criticism. It will pass and be replaced, which is how we learn to relate to all emotion now. None are a life sentence, unless we make them so. As pure energy forms, we encounter it/them, and allow for flow.

Notice for yourself if the emotional pain still feels as it did? Does it still hold you hostage? Did you survive?

This is where the transmutation occurs. As Tolle explained, the energy that it took us to keep this pain locked up is now released and becomes fuel for our presence and growth.

I've done this practice many times since first experiencing it. Sometimes it is easier, sometimes not, but each time is a different ride. It has taught me a lot about where the current state of my emotions originated, and I've become able, although not every time, to make sense where none was available before. It can take a lot of practice to allow yourself to fully experience this type of work.

Words fail me when I try to describe my experience with the work. And, my experience is going to be innately different from yours. Thus, I will refrain from even trying so as not to frame for you what you will experience. But I will say this, that the more you release to the practice, the more you will gain from it. Clarity and relationship to that which we fear will yield a gift that can only be given from oneself, to oneself.

To truly come into right relationship with our emotional spectrum holds within it a simple confidence and mastery of who and what we truly are.

A few more words about pain, the pain-body, and our emotions. The sages of the ages have taught that there are only two basic emotions, love and fear, each at one end of the emotional spectrum and that all others are derivations of these primal two. However, may I ask you to consider what lies under fear itself?

When fear presents itself, isn't it a primal and instinctual reaction to something being threatened in our lives, like our safety for example? We experience fear when our relationships are threatened, or our survival is threatened, our families are threatened, our happiness is threatened. That's because we love our relationships, our families, our survival, and our happiness. And, if we lost those things, we would be in pain and we fear pain in all of its forms. Thus, under our fear, is a deeper current of energy, that of love. So doesn't it follow then, that we feel fear only when something we love is threatened, or we wouldn't feel fear?

Thus, I would venture to say that there is only ONE primal emotion and all others are a derivation of, or reaction to that one, which is Love.

With this in mind, a venture to meet our pain can be catalyzed with the understanding that ultimately under the deepest depth of our pain, is pure and pristine Love. This makes our journey even more important, and even bearable.

Breathe....

Back to our story.

Dante and Virgil meet Plutus, a demon of the Underground. Plutus menaces them by calling for Satan. Virgil, who continues to protect Dante comforts him and says,

"Let not thy fear Harm thee;
for any power that he may have
Shall not prevent thy going down this crag."

Circle of Greed

Here saw I people, more than elsewhere, many,
On one side and the other, with great howls,
Rolling weights forward by main force of chest.

They clashed together, and then at that point
Each one turned backward, rolling retrograde,
Crying, "Why keepest?" and, "Why squanderest thou?"
                    Dante's Inferno, Canto VII

In the 4th Circle, Dante is watching an eternal jousting match. There are two sides against each other, one the avaricious, or hoarders, and one the prodigal and squanderers. The weapons against the other, were huge bags of fortune pushed with their chests. They pushed, then pulled against the other side in everlasting conflict.

This is an interesting dynamic that is innate to our human nature. No longer does our avarice stay confined within ourselves, it now involves others. It is the dynamic of push and pull. Virgil describes the active component of Greed, where we are either one who takes of others, or one who wastes or lavishes upon others at our personal expense.
In relating this to our spiritual pilgrimage, I asked myself, "where would these qualities and dynamics necessarily become a harm to myself or others?"
Obviously, by being a greedy individual we can be labeled as wrong. And, in the sense where I over-save my fortune, or over-spend my fortune, it could be good or bad, depending on many factors. By hoarding, we stop the natural and healthy flow of energy between us and others. Conversely, by pushing or wasting our own energy upon others, we too have created an unhealthy flow of naturally occurring relational energy.

For our expedition into our psyche, both are damaging to ourselves and others. The 'pushing' of parts of our self, projects that which we believe doesn't belong inside us, onto another.
The 'pulling' of someone else's self into our own, makes us a fraud or an imitation of something we are not, and at worst a thief.

This is the entrance gate to our Shadow, or more likely, many of them.

Every person on this planet has a Shadow, and usually many of them. Think of your Shadow Selves as the collection of parts of you and your psyche that have been suppressed, denied, and shunned by your conscious mind and ego.

Carl Jung, a famous psychotherapist from the early-to-mid 1900s, who coined the term 'Shadow' said, "Until you make the unconscious conscious, it will direct your life and you will call it fate." He called our Shadow our 'dark side'.

Our ego, when in a wounded state, creates personas or masks, to hide the most 'unacceptable' parts of ourselves from others so that we can belong. These masks even hide these parts from our conscious mind. These masks are a form of prison, our underworld.

And, as every human does, when these Shadows remain unmet, we push them outside of ourselves by projecting them onto others. This is our spendthrift if you will, where we are vomiting our internalized and seemingly shameful darknesses onto others so we don't have to own them.

When we hoard, or take what is not ours, we create within ourselves a false persona, to paint over our Shadows so that we feel better about what we believe is shameful inside us. We steal what we like from others, and present that mask to the world, yet another form of prison.

For example, some socially visual masks that we are all familiar with are:

The Bully
The Good Girl
The Intellect
The Seductress
The Cool Dude

During my own journey for example, I learned very young that I was more serious than the other children. I didn't like to play, because I didn't understand how to, at least the way that they did. And from that, I developed this idea that I wasn't acceptable to my early tribe. So, I created a dangerous, albeit creative and useful shapeshifter.

Meet my Chameleon. She changes and shifts to be whatever she believes you want her to look like, or be like. And, she worked very well for me for decades, until she didn't.

She was born out of necessity when I didn't fit in. I had started to lock up my 'ashamed of' parts which as you will see later, became covert Shadows that I projected generously onto others, harshly and judgmentally. Then I replaced my 'ashamed of' parts with stolen personality traits from others and paraded them as my own. I created my Chameleon which had to be protected at all costs. We all do this to some degree.

Over many years my layering of pilfered skins became miles thick, and my authentic skin so deeply buried that it no longer existed, which of course was my ego's goal. I had also so forcibly buried the authentic colors of my own skin, that once I exposed my virgin skin to the light, it was pale, over-sensitive, and frail. I was unrecognizable, raw, and easily burned.

The incessant 'push' and 'pull' dynamic creates an utterly confusing chasm between our Prison and our Palace. I thought I had evicted the rightful, albeit ugly and unwanted, tenants from my Palace, and locked up the pretty and smart kidnapped hostages safely in my Prison. All the while, the real prisoners in the dungeon, were my own royal court.

To add more confusion to my Palace, my Royal Council had become Prison Guards, with one purpose. To protect the façade of the Prison, and convince anyone who visits that it looks like a Palace. And it all started as the misunderstanding of a very young girl, who simply wanted to play in her own way.

My example doesn't include the increased damage done when there are severe and traumatic circumstances that happen to so many, such as parental divorce, abuse, or incest. Once these factors are added, the moat of protection becomes so dark and filled with filth, that it seems uncrossable.

But, a crossing is possible.

We need to lighten up our bags of fortune, our bags of fool's gold, one bag at a time. Paradoxically, just as our emotional energies can transmute into greater Presence, each bag of fortune which, when released from the eternal tug-of-war, opens to yield it was always filled.... with our own pure and very real gold. This gold has rightfully and Divinely always been our own.

Furthermore, when we release our prisoners, we no longer have need for the guards at the gates, and our guards are released to shine as our beloved Royal Court once again. Confused? Yes, I was too at first.

Basically, we have created enemies of our true friends, our basic natures, by shaming them into exile. And, we have deployed even more of our natural energies into keeping the prison locked down while we stole our outer identity from others. Releasing each part of our nature to be what it was meant to be, releases an enormous amount of rightful, authentic, and Divine energy.

Our next practice then, has two goals. Beneath the intensely creative energy invested to hold the prison walls together and guard the prison gate to hide our deception lies the energy to preserve the façade of not having an internal prison of Shadows in the first place. Can you imagine what I, or you, could do with a release of that much creative energy? That's goal one.

The second goal is to tear down the prison and free every creature we have locked up. You see, in accepting all of who we are, the good, bad, and ugly, we become whole no matter what. Being whole means no more stealth attacks from the dark recesses of our saboteur, the Shadow. In doing so, we liberate them from their dungeon, and they transmute into trusted companions.

Rumi, the epic 13th-century Iranian poet, looks at being whole and bringing home these disowned parts of ourselves in his beautiful poem, The Guest House.

The Guest House

This being human is a guest house.
Every morning a new arrival.
A joy, a depression, a meanness,
some momentary awareness comes
as an unexpected visitor.
Welcome and entertain them all!
Even if they are a crowd of sorrows,
who violently sweep your house
empty of its furniture,
still, treat each guest honorably.
He may be clearing you out
for some new delight.
The dark thought, the shame, the malice.
meet them at the door laughing and invite them in.
Be grateful for whatever comes.
because each has been sent
as a guide from beyond.

One of my personal experiences with transmutation is one that I used to be hesitant to talk about, until I was able to fully discharge the shameful energy around it. And shame is for me one of the most powerful emotions that I experience. Shame has driven me to my most harmful and self-destructive behaviors.

When I was a young teenage white girl, going to a non-white school where I experienced severe ethnic discrimination, I began my 'acting out' phase. It was the birth time of one of my more colorful Chameleon skins, Dora the Dirty Whore.

She had been birthed near the time of my teenage encounter with the boys trying to molest me behind the school. Somehow, I learned how powerful this young, sexual energy was, and I twisted it to my advantage. She became a 'tool' to deploy. And, Dora was born.

She became the 'skin' I needed to get attention, at a time in my life where any attention, other than schoolyard bullying and physical violence, was welcomed. The emotional sensation attached to her was that of a life savior. Dora would show up when I longed for attention. Deploying Dora with the boys made their attention easy to grab. And, I found that if I allowed Dora to pick my clothes, and put my makeup on just right, even the girls started to accept me as one of them.

She was a fast and efficient fix that visited for the next 25 years, and she made herself at home in times where I experienced emotional neediness. She was always at my beck and call if I was lonely. But, healthy she was not.

By using the techniques I describe below, I unearthed her, visited her, and befriended her. In that transmutation, her original nature was reborn. She became who I know now as, Michelle, my Mystic Lover. She had initially been that in her first moments of creation, in early adolescence when my sexual identity was being formed. But she had become a toxic version of my innocent sexuality after years of misunderstanding and negligence. She had morphed into Dora, the Dirty Whore.

I've reconciled the needs of Dora, and she has grown up. And now I invite Michelle to visit quite often. My husband looks forward to her visits as well.

This is an example of transmutation. It's also a way of seeing that all of our Shadows have light and dark, sinner and saint. Our Universe has a mysterious way of keeping everything in balance. Yin cannot exist without Yang, you can't understand happy unless you have felt sad, light can't be understood until we meet darkness. And, our Shadow is also just a fallen Angel.

You have probably heard someone say, "What you resist, persists." This is exactly what happens when we don't face our Shadow. They can be like petulant children until they are acknowledged and befriended. And, in some cases, maybe they can't be transmuted, but simply accepted for who they are, even if they are not exactly angelic.

On the other hand, there are many situations where our Shadow is made of Gold, and we have suppressed our shine to shrink away from our brilliance. Many suppressions can be those personality traits that we hold back to not outshine others, because again, we are ultimately wanting to belong. Unearthing these Golden Shadows, fortunately, follow the same steps.

So, how do we meet and befriend these illusive Shadows? This can be a multiple-step process. And it begins by becoming curious about the trail of tears they've left behind. Our Shadows reveal themselves as Projection, and have usually left behind some damage or tears.

We begin by paying attention to our reactions. Our reactions that hold some sense of 'charge' will guide us to where we project.

Take a stroll, turn on the TV, or even better just sit and do some personal inquiry and honest reflection. Sit and think about those times when you were highly emotional at someone or something, for example, times when you felt angry, jealous, righteous, discounted, or ashamed. Any times of conflict that you've been in with another is a great place to start.

In times of turmoil within ourselves and others, we are projecting our inner turmoil onto our external environment. Projection is, again, the process of seeing our disowned aspects of ourselves within others, the proverbial 'push'. When this disowned aspect is buried deeply enough as Shadow, it is projected with an emotional 'charge'. This is the clue to finding Shadow, by examining where and when we have felt a charge towards someone else, whether or not you have acted on it.

> This is how we make our list of Shadows to look at.
> Examine your level of emotional reaction to:
> Political Groups
> Boss / Co-Workers
> Sexual orientations
> Drivers on the highway
> Hatreds
> Biases / prejudices
> Fat people, dumb people, pretty people, ugly people, rich people….
> Lucy, George, Alice, whoever you deeply dislike

The key is to make a very honest list. No matter how silly you "think" something might be, if it makes you angry, jealous, outraged, resentful, whatever BIG emotion it evokes, PUT IT ON YOUR LIST.

Carl Jung said, "Projection makes the whole world a replica of our unknown face."

Now, pick one item or person from your list.

Projection Practice:

This is going to feel very strange, and it should. It's probably going to hurt, and it should. If you hear a voice inside saying, "No way, not true, no, not me," then you're onto something and doing it right.

Carl Jung also said, "Everything that irritates us about others can lead us to an understanding of ourselves."

This practice works especially well when doing it with a trusted friend. You can do this alone as well, but it works better with someone. In any case, obtain a hand-held mirror. Find a quiet place with no disruptions from the outside world. Sit down and do some relaxation breathing to begin.

If you have a friend then their instructions are easy. They are to hold space. This means no speaking, facial expressions, or touching. Holding space is actually difficult to do well, as it means that someone is to be there 'energetically'. They are there to support you by witnessing you and your work, holding the knowing and confidence that you are capable of making it through this <u>on your own</u>. That is ALL, it does not mean save you, humor you, nod to support your victim, show sympathy, NOTHING ELSE.

I call holding space, "seeing the Divine" in another.

3rd Person
1. Picture the person, group, or situation you've chosen to practice with. Build up your emotion around this person or persons. Replay the interaction(s).
2. When you are really feeling the charged emotion, begin by telling your friend (or the <u>back</u> of the mirror) about

"your story" in 3rd person as if you're telling a friend...really let loose and include, for example:
   a. What your feeling. (ex. "I'm really pissed off!")
   b. Your judgments, why you feel the way you do. (ex. "She has no shame! She treated me like a friend, and the whole time she planned to stab me in the back! She.....")
3. Sum it up with, "She/He/They is/are _____. (ex. "She is a back-stabbing bitch!")

Take a few clearing breaths, and imagine your friend, or the back of the mirror, <u>AS</u> this person/persons.

2nd Person

In 2nd person language (which will be lots of "you did, you said, you are"), speak directly to them and tell them just how you feel and why. At the end of your rant, say the same conclusion you did above, but in 2nd person. Ex. "You are a back-stabbing bitch!" Don't hold back...

When you (your ranting) are complete, take some cleansing, relaxing breaths.

Finally, turn your attention towards yourself. Have your friend hold the mirror, or you hold it. Face your image in the mirror.

1st Person

Speaking the same steps and conclusion, in <u>first-person</u> language towards yourself repeat it 3-5 times and feel into it deeply. Example:
   "I am really pissed off!" or maybe even, "I have really pissed you off!"
   "I have no shame! I've treated her like a friend, and the whole time I had planned on stabbing her in the back!"

"I am a back-stabbing bitch."

Sit with this a while. Be willing to explore the possibility that there is some truth to this. No need to rush this, in fact, don't! Talk with your friend, or your reflection, and explore…..when have I acted this way to others. Deeply FEEL into it. Does it elicit a feeling in your body, a sensation of sorts, can you actually describe it?

The key is the exploration itself. What you've accomplished here, is to open up to a new possibility, one which you may have had suppressed, locked in the dungeon. Let it out...and be compassionate towards this part of yourself.

Be willing to EXPLORE the possibility that this is actually is a part of you. And if it is, then 'pull' it back and own that this is a part of who you are, or can be at times, or behave like, or....

This practice is a version of a process created by Ken Wilbur, founder of Integral Theory. He calls it the 3-2-1 process. He explains that the reason this process of going from 3rd person, to 2nd, then 1st works, is that this is the reversing of the process that created the projection in the first place.

We first took the shameful aberration and buried it deeply inside ourselves. Then, we turned it onto other individuals, then onto general judgments of groups of others. Look around, you see this happening to everyone around you, it is easy to see in others. It is much more complex to see in ourselves.

Now, we walk the path backward, the 3-2-1, to re-own it. Bring it home.

You may run across some parts that you can't stomach to own, can't believe are yours. But, I assure you that we cannot see anything in others that we do not also possess at some level. The ego-self will fight this fiercely.

And don't forget the Gold... have you ever noticed just how thoughtful someone was, or how charismatic someone is? I assure you, that you own that too! Not too surprisingly, there are a lot of us that discovered at some point in our lives that our Gold, meaning our strengths, intelligence, passions, etc. were maybe too brilliant for others, so we've toned it down. We have shunned our own light. We have hidden our Gold, just as deeply as our Shadow. Go through the same process and bring them home too.

This is one of my favorite writings of all time, about our Golden Shadows, written by Marianne Williamson:

Our Deepest Fear

Our deepest fear is not that we are inadequate. Our deepest fear is that we are powerful beyond measure. It is our light, not our darkness that most frightens us.

We ask ourselves, Who am I to be brilliant, gorgeous, talented, and fabulous? Actually, who are you not to be?

You are a child of God. Your playing small does not serve the world. There is nothing enlightened about shrinking so that other people will not feel insecure around you. We are all meant to shine, as children do.

We were born to make manifest the glory of God that is within us. It is not just in some of us; it is in everyone and as we let our own light shine, we unconsciously give others permission to do the same.

As we are liberated from our own fear, our presence automatically liberates others.

At this point in our work on Shadow, know that there is more to be (un)done with Shadows. All we have done thus far, is uncover that they do exist and how we push and pull pieces of our psyche in and out of others.

But, to do the ultimate work of meeting them in person, we need yet another dive closer to where they live, for they reside deeper in the Inferno, and we have yet to reach their depths. I promise that we will, but to reach that depth, we need to survive the descent through the City of Dis, which lies on the next horizon. And to reach Dis, we must first traverse the swampy, stinking waters of the River Styx.

Circle of Wrath

And I, who stood intent upon beholding,
Saw people mudbesprent in that lagoon,
All of them naked and with angry look.

They smote each other not alone with hands,
But with the head and with the breast and feet,
Tearing each other piecemeal with their teeth.

Dante's Inferno, Canto VII

In the final Circle of Upper Hell, Dante sees 'Shades' (souls or Shadows) crouched on the bank of the River Styx. They are covered in mud, and strike and bite one another. These are the

Wrathful, those who were consumed with anger throughout their mortal lives.

Virgil walks Dante through the hoards until they come to a tall tower whose pinnacle is bursting with flames. There, they encounter the boatman, Phlegyas, the rageful and impetuous.

Virgil has to convince Phlegyas to ferry the mortal Dante across. They leave the shore only to find the waters of the river crowded with more of the damned, but these beings are submerged within the foulness of the vile river. These are the Sullen, whose anger choked them in life. For all eternity, they are now damned to gurgle, unable to express themselves, for the anger that continues to choke them.

> *Beneath the water people are who sigh*
> *And make this water bubble at the surface,*
> *As the eye tells thee wheresoe'er it turns.*
>
> *Fixed in the mire they say, 'We sullen were*
> *In the sweet air, which by the sun is gladdened,*
> *Bearing within ourselves the sluggish reek;*
>
> *Now we are sullen in this sable mire.'*
> *This hymn do they keep gurgling in their throats,*
> *For with unbroken words they cannot say it."*
>
> Dante's Inferno, Canto VII

Wrath and anger are amongst the most destructive emotions when we have given our rage free access to come and go as it pleases. Although anger itself isn't destructive at all. In fact, it can be a very healthy emotion to get to know and live with.

Our primary emotion of anger is simply an emotional response to something we perceive as a threat. It can be utilized in many healthy ways. For example, it allows us to be assertive when boundaries need to be held. It allows the Mother Bear to protect her young.

But, use our anger to destruct we do, or rather, our anger uses us. There are many ways that we abuse this emotion. We can abuse it outwardly if we perceive threats incorrectly for example, and our anger can be triggered for the wrong reason. Or, we might misjudge something as threatening when it's not.

The most destructive use of anger is when it is allowed to express itself without any limitation in its expression, and this can easily erupt into violence in its most extreme.

Inwardly, unexpressed emotions can harm our health and wellbeing. Anger can be an insidious toxin that eats away at our ability to see things clearly, and then to accept them the way they are.

Thus, we want to look deeper at how we either suppress our anger, which turns into resentment, or how we express our anger in unhealthy ways. Let's do both.

There is an added benefit to this next practice. It works very effectively with any emotion. In fact, it works with all of our emotions, both suppressed and over-emotive. And, even better, it works when they are all active at the same time, inwardly and outwardly.

We are building upon the pulling back of Projection from the Circle of Greed. There, we began to uncover the existence of the hostages locked in the dungeon. Now we will unlock the door and introduce ourselves. Here, in the Circle of Wrath, we are taking a greater risk, to actually enter the most guarded of prison cells.

Calling Inner Voices Practice

This method was first introduced to me by a wonderful Zen-minded man. In its original form, it was designed by Hal and Sidra Stone as a method of dialoguing with our inner voices, our hostages, and our prisoners. These inner voices though, are simply expressions of your inner selves, personas, and emotive guises.

These expressions, or inner voices, are coming from under the surface of the consciousness. This practice is a way of allowing and even inviting into conversation those deeper expressions, and bringing them to the surface. We allow them space to express and be as they are, unabashedly.

Let me describe this practice by way of a personal example.

I am in my second marriage now and it is to a man that has made his own way out of the dark as well. He is in what I lovingly call his Sacred Masculine most of the time. And, because we are both doing our best to live consciously and pursue our own growth relentlessly, I do believe we were brought together to intensify our growth. However, this means that he and I push each other's buttons…..a lot. Over time, an undercurrent grew from the unexpressed angers, resentments, and frustrations. This undercurrent nearly cost us our marriage.

As I needed space after what I felt was very probably the final battle, I went to a lake and sat next to the shore. The cacophony of voices in my head felt like there must have been 20 people in there, all arguing about how to handle the situation at hand. I felt absolutely schizophrenic with the constant stream of the multitude of thoughts all being triggered at once, each resounding loudly within the confines of my head.

I'm sure you recognize this, we've all had many voices inside our head and when they get to talking all at the same time, it's quite annoying and confusing. I used to feel that it was just the jumble of all my thoughts tying themselves in knots and I was just not emotionally mature enough to handle situations because of it. This turned out to not be the case at all. I just needed a tool to use to untangle the voices.

Another example of when we hear these voices, is when we are making decisions and we can't make up our mind. We have opposing thoughts about it. Or, when we have more than one feeling all at the same time. I didn't know if I was crazy, or just indecisive to the point of being totally dysfunctional.

I discovered with Inner Voice Dialogue, that each of those voices is a legitimate part of me, and each a different expression of my psyche. They each have been given birth at some point in my life, conception or otherwise, in response to an emotional experience. Some are my nature, some are defense mechanisms, and some are just part of being human.

Sitting there that fateful day, I took out a pad of paper and pen. I tried to calm myself down a bit with some deep breathing, and then shifted my position. Then, I listened for the first emotional voice to speak. It turned out to be Sad Sally. And I let her write, all that she wanted to, no matter how silly Sally might sound. She had the floor, and I gave her all the time she needed to say everything she wanted.

She cried, until her nose ran down her face, in sobs that seemed as though they wouldn't stop. Eventually, they did. I asked her if there was anything left that she wanted to say right now. Wiping her nose, she said, "No."

I took a few more breaths once Sally said she was done, and then I shifted my legs underneath me. And I listened again.

And, it was no surprise to me, that Angry Alice was the next to want to talk. Talk? No, actually she yells a lot. I let her yell all over her own page, then the next, and then the next. Apparently, she had a lot to get out of her system.

Next up was Chloe Co-Dependent. She's all about fixing things, and making sure that no one is angry. She filled a whole page with a litany of ways to say, "I'm sorry." Did you know that can be said in about 136,748 ways? She got very creative!

What's important to embrace here, is that I am giving each inner voice the space, and my undivided attention. And more importantly, the honor of saying anything and everything she wants to. Nothing was judged, criticized, justified, or even discussed. Each She had her floor.

And not to be sexist, Marvin the Meek had a chance to appear, to continue his normal onslaught in response to my husband's natural charm and social ease. But, he wasn't stirring this time, so no paper needed for him.

If I let my inner Judge (who by the way is named Judge Janis) judge Sally, Alice, or Chloe, each time they speak, then I am showing them dishonor. This does the same to them that dishonor would do to anyone. It makes them defensive and they feel disrespected. However, Judge Janis had some things to say on her own. So, in turn, I gave her the floor. Her page became filled with judgments that filled a scorecard. Right or wrong, I respected her space to express.

When 'they' feel disrespected, they can go underground and become a dangerous and vengeful Shadow. And, when they do, they await any opportunity to covertly escape the darkness into my reality. When they take me by surprise and they have been pent up, they over-release and this is followed by several days of apologies to the others I have allowed them free access to.

As the day progressed, I nearly used up the pad of paper while Mary the Martyr, Veronica the Victim, and even Dora, the Dirty Whore took their turns. There were more, but I think this illustrates the practice.

And, there is still one who has yet to make the most important appearance of all.

First, a couple of really important points here. Yes, after a while of doing this practice, you can build such a deep relationship with these parts of yourself, you can even give them names. It's not crazy; it's honoring that part of myself by doing so.

Also, it's critical to shift your physical position, even if it is very minute, in order to call in or allow the next voice. You might notice that each voice is associated with a definitive feeling in your body as well as its own emotional state. That is who they are, a representation of each part of you, your emotional states, your charged beliefs, everything.

After nearly 3 hours of 'testimony' on the shore that day, it was time to call on....Willow, the Wise One.

In Inner Voice Dialogue, they describe the personas similar to the instruments in an orchestra. Because the individual instruments would be a discord of sounds without an organizing wisdom, they introduce the idea of the Conductor. This brings harmony. It keeps the flutes from trying to be trombones, and violins from being trumpets. My conductor is Willow.

I think of her more as my higher-self, my intuitive voice, my connection to that which is greater than I, my connection to the Divine. Willow had listened very attentively to each part of me speak that day. She honored each by giving them all of the space they needed to express themselves completely.

And, she was able to then bring a level of clarity to what had been an endless cacophony of confusion and noise. Now, I knew what had to be said and done. In fact, the clarity in going through this process is so profound, that once your 'conductor' begins to orchestrate each instrument, I find that there is no doubt whatsoever, no undischarged emotion, and therefore no remaining drama. There is only clear, unbiased, compassionate, Truth.

This example of the Inner Voice Dialogue practice can be extremely powerful in multiple ways. It's not meant just to be an exercise of gaining clarity when you find yourself in conflict. More importantly, it's meant to get into touch with those parts of you that create drama, judge, rage, self-criticize, play victim, be resentful, and so much more.

You can begin with any conflict you have in your life. It's natural to feel silly at first, letting some part of you just go and say whatever it wants. Your 'Self-Critic' may show up to judge you for doing something silly. Your 'Controller' may show up to control and put a stop to the situation. Your 'Judge' may show up to blame everyone else. Let them, but make them each wait their turn, no interrupting.

Listen closely when you do this. Listen with your body for the faintest of emotions, and invite them to the surface to speak. Treat them like your children, for they are. They show up at your door for a touch of compassion and wanting to be fed, bathed, heard, and most importantly, loved.

Your goal is to build a new relationship with these denied parts of yourself. They are not going away, so give them space and get to know them.

In the teachings of the Medicine Wheel, we have rounded the South tip, the Lodge of Introspection. In the Vedic text, the Bhagavad Gita, we have revealed our emotions. In the teachings of the Tao te Ching, we have begun to detach from our emotional attachments. In the 12-Step Program, we have completed Steps 1-3 and parts of 4. We continue to follow the Golden Thread of all of these.

Dante and Virgil have now survived all of the Circles of Upper Hell where the Shades were condemned because of, what Dante called, their Daliances of Indulged Passion.

For us, our blinders are off. We now have the ability to introspect, and we are developing inner sight. We no longer blindly dally in our indulgences. I hope I've provided a few tools and guides to help us endure the remaining sojourns of our pilgrimage.

Where we and Dante are heading is Lower Hell, where the offenses and eternal punishments grow in severity. The entrance into Lower Hell lies within the walls of the City of Dis. As they approach, they are accosted by a band of fallen angels called the three Furies, who are half woman, half serpent.

Where in a moment saw I swift uprisen
The three infernal Furies stained with blood,
Who had the limbs of women and their mien,

And with the greenest hydras were begirt;
Small serpents and cerastes were their tresses,
Wherewith their horrid temples were entwined.
                              Dante's Inferno, Canto IX

Lower Hell: Circles of Violence and Fraud

The three Furies historically represent evil deeds, thoughts, and words. They are the avengers and tormentors of the underworld and eternally search for those who are deserving of damnation. When they see Dante, they call upon their master, the famed Medusa, to turn Dante into stone. Virgil tells Dante to shield his eyes and suddenly they are saved by an unnamed Angel, who forces the Gates of Dis to be opened to Virgil and his mortal friend, Dante.

The furies in our tale are threatening Dante's entrance to Dis, which Virgil has been unable to obtain on his own. Is not this similar to the guards of the prison gate, the reaction of a threatened ego, where it calls upon tormentors to lower one's confidences? And if they are not enough by themselves, they call on the ultimate mistress of fear, that of Medusa, Queen of the underground. She whose tresses are a crown of snakes, whose face will turn a man to stone. Is this not the archetypal resonance of the royal executioner?

And what of the Unnamed Angel, who swoops in, dispatches the Furies, and opens the Gates of Dis? Could this have some connection to our alter-ego, that part of us that knows what is best for us, our guardian angel, our higher power, that which cannot be named? Here, we start to see that Virgil is less of a savior for Dante, and that Dante is starting to have to rely less on Virgil than on something else, not yet nameable, but absolutely necessary.

This is the final Gate into a world that Dante can never return through. He has only one way to exit, and to exit, he must go all the way through. Such is our path as well.

In this Lower landscape of the Inferno, there are three Circles before the final destination where Satan lives. Each Circle has inner circles and these further segregate who the sin was cast against in life; for example, self, others, or God. Luckily, we'll be able to combine some of these Circles (a small but generous consolation for having survived thus far) and travel through a few at a time.

Virgil explains that these sins are considered more harshly in their condemnation because they violate the very design of the Divine. He explains that there are only two sources of real wealth in the Universe, that of Nature, and that of Art or creative source-energy.

What I understand this to mean, is that once my own transgressions violate the Divine rights of another being, I have penance to make.

Atonement.

Circle of Heresy

The sepulchres make all the place uneven;
So likewise did they there on every side,
Saving that there the manner was more bitter;

For flames between the sepulchres were scattered,
By which they so intensely heated were,
That iron more so asks not any art.

All of their coverings uplifted were,
And from them issued forth such dire laments,
Sooth seemed they of the wretched and tormented.

Dante's Inferno, Canto X

In the sixth Circle and approaching the City, Dante finds himself being led through a valley of open, confusedly scattered and flaming tombs. Each tomb holds thousands of lost souls, condemned to the fiery heat, who lament wretchedly and tormentedly. Their tombs will finally be closed at the end of time, completing their final sentence that reflects their denial of life after death. The Shades within the scorching sepulchers are those who were Heretics in life, having committed the sin of denying or violating the Divine.

Heresy in this sense is a violation of Divine Law. This can be defined in a multitude of ways. But the easiest of all, and one that every tradition agrees on, is the Golden Rule, *Do unto others as you would have them do unto you.*

Therefore, no matter what religion, culture, or tradition you come from, we can all agree that the essential Divine Law is to treat each other with respect, empathy, and love. Any transgression against another from this vantage point adds to our Karmic debt.

Unlike the Shades in our story, we have the opportunity to alter our destiny, or Karma, to change our reflection within and without. We have the privilege and Divine Right to change.

We have the Divine Right to be forgiven for our transgressions. But, unlike some theological understandings, or more accurately their misunderstandings, we must take action of some kind to right the wrongs of our past. It is simply not enough, in our pursuit of personal empowerment, to know we've done wrong against another.

One of my favorite ways to deepen my understanding of human nature is to study mythology. In Hindu mythology, there is a Tantric story of Shiva and Shakti that I love. Shiva is described as pure Divine Consciousness. He is the unlimited, unswayable, and unchanging observer. He is the Father of the Universe, the formlessness of consciousness.

Shakti, is everything energy, power, change, nature and movement. She brings formlessness into form, manifests consciousness into life. She is the Mother of the Universe, and it is only through Her that the formless becomes form. Therefore, the Father is the Father of the Mother, and the Mother is the Mother of the Father. They coexist, and one cannot Be without the Other.

One without the other means either a world of consciousness alone, or a world of form without consciousness. It is only in the Divine Union of Shiva and Shakti that form and formlessness bring forth a world where we, as creatures of the Universe, can live with purpose. It is the ultimate goal of our journey, the marrying of a higher degree of consciousness manifesting itself in our living, the co-creation of our life.

Relating this to our Dante world and atonement means that not only must we awaken to consciousness, but we must actively live accordingly. When we do, we actively pursue some remedy that brings us into right relationship with Divine Law. We pursue Shiva mind, and live it through Shakti energy.

We must take an action. With this taking of action, we take responsibility for our harms and whether or not the other person forgives us, we can at least find forgiveness for ourselves. And, I believe the Universal powers that be, call them what you will, forgive us too.

Going further still, understand that penance, or atonement, is not a punishment. The use of punishment upon another evades the premise of atonement which is the recognition that we have actually done wrong and we own it. It is our cosmic or mystic responsibility. Without this, personal growth will stop right here, and becomes self-seeking narcissism which a form of spiritual hypocrisy. For, we are not meant to be 'right', but be 'just' in our loving, empathetic relationship with all other inhabitants of our Universe, sentient and non-sentient. This is the basis of living in right-relationship.

Thus, simply, we seek to clean up our past and do our best to be, now and forever, better in all relationships, internally and externally.

There is much symbolism in this Canto that can help point our way. First is the indication that Virgil is becoming less and less able to protect Dante. I fathom this to mean that I as an individual, must start to take more responsibility for my own learning. This comes as a 'non-negotiable' once we entered the first Gate of the Inferno. It also relates to our ability to begin to trust our own selves.

Once my awakening began in earnest, there was no turning back, no blaming others any longer. I was solely responsible for my feelings and emotions once I started understanding my own demons. And, the deeper I explore, the more I realize I am my own co-Creator of my reality; I and I alone. I may not be fully responsible for where I find myself, although I could argue that to some extent. But, I am responsible for how I show up.

The Furies that Dante met at the Gate to Dis, could be harbingers of yet more unearthing left to do. And, the presence of the menacing half-serpentine women suggest that if I were to stop here, I would be turned to stone. Again, I've come too far to go back now without even worse consequences in my life.

The open casket lids and the torment of being engulfed in flames for all eternity is representative of the undying torment we inflict upon ourselves by consciously living with the knowledge of our unrepaired transgressions against other Divine creatures.

Given the sole responsibility to be in just-relationship and the knowledge that until we make atonement things will get worse, do what must be done. We may not always have Virgil by our side to call upon the Heavens and open Gates. We must be able to stand steadily, affronted by the threats of the Furies, alone and readily penitent.

And, because I've visited this Circle before, I'm going to recommend we take the next few steps slowly.

Let's start with how Heaven administers its damnation.

Fire

We tend to misunderstand fire. Fire has been misunderstood to be destructive. However, this is not how Nature uses it. Mother Nature uses fire as a renewal mechanism when she thins out overgrown or diseased forests, for example. Fire is, in its very nature, alchemical. It changes what it touches. It is change in and of itself; as it ignites it changes from heat to something that is not matter, nor energy. It is a combination of both.

Many, and I would venture to say All, cultures throughout time have used fire in healing rituals in some way. We can too.

Jumping Over the Fire Ceremony

Start to make a list of transgressions that you have made in your past. Start simply, by listing those who you have wronged. We'll expand on this list in a later Circle.

For each person or situation, dedicate a separate piece of paper. Then list the transgressions and learnings gained from each.

It's important to identify what someone or something has taught you. You will see why in a minute.

Find a safe place to have a small and safe fire. Maybe use a fire-safe bowl, or small outdoor fire-ring. Do this in as reverent a manner as you can. Consider this fire ceremonial and sacred.

Begin by speaking some words, prayers, invocations, to the flames, and ask them to be a sacred witness to your sincerity, release, and vow.

1. Read one sheet at a time. Feel each transgression and the emotions it elicits. Then, feel the gratitude for each lesson you've been blessed to receive.
    a. As you read the lessons learned to the fire, make a vow to bring the lesson into your consciousness, and live that lesson in your life. Do so, IN HONOR OF/TO _____ (who you transgressed against).
2. Hold these vows in your heart, with full sincerity to honor each, on behalf of those teachers (those you have harmed).
3. Then, burn the paper (s).
4. After all sheets have been burned, jump over the fire, holding these vows in your heart.

This sweet, earnest ceremony comes from many cultures. For example, the Persians and Celts 'jump the fire' for luck, vow taking, crop fertility, and all sorts of reasons. The flames are seen as alchemical elements of Heaven and Earth and by jumping through the smoke, your prayers are carried to the God(s).

And, as with any Ceremony, you will get out of it what you bring into it. Reverence is the key. If it simply doesn't strike you as something you can do with any seriousness, then don't. As with any practice in this book, do what you feel resonates for you, and leave the rest.

In 12-Step work, this is considered a 'Living Amends', which means, that you are actively vowing to bring the lessons from others into your life, while honoring them, personally, for bestowing upon you those lessons. Every transgression provides an opportunity for learning and growth.

It is actually the vow and the honoring of your 'teacher' or 'grantor' of that lesson that is so powerful. It works wonderfully for those that may have passed on or are no longer part of your life.

And, know this; once you have made this vow, the Universe, God, Goddess, Allah, your Higher Power, whoever, has heard your vows. Live accordingly, as the Furies are never far away, anxious to turn you into stone.

You need not live in fear of eternal damnation in the next world. In fact, I don't really think it is filled with such eternal torment as Dante's world, but living in this life is still in front of you. Hell is what you make it, and with atonement as a tool, and fire as a friend, it need not be as painful as we are taught that it is. Your inner world is full enough of demons, you need not add any more.

And we're not done yet. We are now going to take Atonement to the next level and really rev it up. We are going to bring more Shakti energy to this critical phase. We are going to add even more action!

Circle of Violence

But fix thine eyes below; for draweth near
The river of blood, within which boiling is
Whoe'er by violence doth injure others."
                    Dante's Inferno, Canto XII

Dante and Virgil attempt to enter Circle 7, the Circle of Violence, and are met by the Minotaur, the Infamy of Crete. As the Minotaur gnaws his own flesh, Virgil tries to convince him to allow them safe passage. But the Minotaur charges, and they are forced to run down a rocky hillside, barely escaping certain carnage and violence, and narrowly enter the Circle safely.

They make their way further down the hillside inside the Circle's entrance, to the River Phlegethon, which is a boiling river of blood and fire. Centaurs, half man and half horse, stand on the bank shooting arrows. They shoot at any soul who attempts to escape the bloody currents.

Virgil explains that the souls here are condemned to wallow in blood, as they did in life.

Thus begins their travels through the landscape in the Seventh Circle. This is the first inner Circle, where violence was committed against others.

Dante and Virgil also visit the inner circles where offenders waged violence against themselves, and then against Nature and Creation-Art. The perpetrators of self-violence are damned to live their afterlife as gnarled, thorny trees. They are fed on by Harpies, which are hideous clawed birds with the faces of women. This represents their disrespect for their mortal bodies in life, thus they are taken away from them in death.

The sinners against Nature and Creation-Art wander forever in the great Plain of Burning Sand, scorched by great flakes of flame falling from the sky. They are fated to live without any possibility of beauty to ever surround them again.

All of these inner Circles have one thing in common. They are the interminable dwelling place of those who inflicted violence. It could be said that every Circle we have visited thus far has perpetuated some degree of violence, even if it was just within us and hadn't escaped inner confines to affect other people yet.

We are now focused, however, on the deepening of our awakening and pursuit of personal betterment. We wish to be whole by continuing to cultivate a deeper understanding of all of who we are. By now, we have come a long way in building more conscious relationships with our stories, personalities, and emotions. As reward for your valiant and courageous efforts to survive this far, I offer practices that take us even deeper yet.

Beginning in the last chapter, we are aiming to build more conscious relationships with those people who are part of our past. We do this in order to be better 'relators' to those in our present and our future.

According to the 12-Step philosophy, making peace with our past is part of our recovery, and I posit that this is a big difference between the thoroughness of the 12-Step and other methodologies. Not all of the other methods believe that this revisitation and 'active' atonement is necessary. Having lived the 12 Step method, I view this next step as a must, and can be the most painful step. In fact, the next two steps can be arduous and lifelong.

It involves more Shakti, more action, more atonement.

The intensity of the imagery in our travels through the Inferno continue to offer us more breadcrumbs that are worth examining.

First, Virgil is completely unable to protect Dante when they meet the Minotaur. They must run into the rock-strewn valley to escape. This isn't to say that our guides have deserted us. But, it emphasizes all the more that we must continue, at any cost, regardless of the danger. There is no way back, only forward. And, being able to act on our own is becoming more and more vital to our survival.

As in all of Dante's Circles, each fate is intimately tied to its infraction. Isn't it true, that when our inner world is violent, our outer world reflects more of the same? It seems that we create our outer reality, or fate, the same as the lot of lost souls we will meet in Dis.

Another interesting item of note, is the change in our landscape, the creation of these inner circles inside the main Circle. It would seem that there is a widening in the perspective of the base infraction and more focus on each level or degree of infraction. Is this synonymous with the idea that there are more and more ways to affect our outer world as the effects of our inner world come from deeper and deeper within? And, that each deserves attentive examination?

Violence can come in many forms, and as we prepare for our next practice, we need to take stock of just how many ways we violate the peace and sanctity of our self, others, and our world.

Violence is a strong word. In the context of personal growth, we could lighten it up to something more like conflict, wounding, or hurts. What I'm talking about are the ones we have created through our own actions. Let's chat about 'scorecarding' for a bit.

Scorecarding is the mental keeping of an inner record of how others have harmed us, or have been deserving of our wrath. To fall prey to this thinking at this stage in our journey would be to take a huge step backward. But going back to meet the Minotaur is not an appealing option.

Here, in this realm, it matters not whether we have been wronged by others. It matters only that we have harmed others with our behavior, period. It doesn't matter who started what; it only matters that we participated in playing the game, whether or not we felt justified at any level. The simple measure is that we participated in a harm against our self, others, or our world.

Participating in conflict, wounding, or hurt/harm, is violent. We can look at times where we have violated someone's Divine Rights, those that we each own, to be happy, whole, and content. When we participate at any level to disrupt or violate these, we have violated Universal or Divine Law.

Even those actions to perpetuate harm to another indirectly is considered a violation. It is energetic at a minimum, like holding resentments against another inside us. It never affects the other directly, but does directly impact our ability to be in right relationship with that person, and directly impacts our own ability to be at peace.

As you build your list of transgressions on others, if there is any doubt as to what belongs on it, simply ask yourself, if the tables were turned, how would you feel about it? Even indirect transgressions like gossip then, would fall onto that list, wouldn't it?

Another way to look at harms is based on the Universal Law of Change. Everything changes, nothing remains still, not even stillness. Therefore, if everything moves either one direction, or another, ask yourself, "Has this behavior or thought moved me closer in right relationship (to myself, others, or my world), or farther away?"

The list of what qualifies can seem daunting, but it doesn't have to be. You can start with the transgressions that stand out for you, the real biggies. They may lead to others, and you may end up doing this more than once in your travails. The only hard and fast rule, is that thorough and painful honesty are musts.

A personal example would be my separation from my first husband. We both had built our relationship around drinking early on, and it hadn't changed for 23 years. Until I got sober. At the time I went through this, I had just finished my stay in

Rehab, and had tried to live back at home with him, to make it work under very different circumstances.

When it became obvious to me that he couldn't or wouldn't follow a path of recovery, I had to leave. Although I feel this had been the right move to make, I have carried a great burden of guilt around this. As his circumstances continued to get worse and worse, leading to jail, homelessness, and eventually death, the guilt grew.

Does this fit as a transgression, my having caused someone great harm by having abandoned our relationship? No, surely not given that it no longer could work given our new dynamic. However, it was how I left the relationship that did belong on my 'list' of harms.

I had chosen to amplify and embellish his harms, on my scorecard, to justify my leaving him. I fed my anger and righteousness to such an extent that it overrode my misplaced guilt, rather than working on the real problem, my guilt itself. And, I stayed very justifiably angry (I thought) for many years, which really only caused me harm in the long run.

My anger had become resentment, which AA says is the surest way back to drinking again. Resentment they like to say, is like feeding yourself poison and expecting the other person to die.

Very unfortunately, his drinking caused his death a few years ago. And, after I had no choice but to face my guilt, was I able to release the resentment. My guilt came from my feelings of not being able to save him and having hurt him deeply, before my own sobriety. This guilt manifested to the extent that I believed it was my fault he digressed so far as to meet his death. It seems so simple now, but not while I was in the throes of the emotional avalanche for many years.

And, I used the Fire Practice from the previous chapter to do a Living Amends. Now, I honor him by having learned gentleness from this man, and I do my best to bring more of it into my life, always in his honor.

And, I had Shadow Work to do on my internalized guilt.

In this example, the important things to note are that in making a list of transgressions, I could bring none of my scorecarded rationalizations into it. I had to own what was mine, legitimately, and what was not. I had to separate the wrongful resentment from the misguided guilt. The resentment belonged on my Harms Inventory towards others per se, but the guilt belonged on my Harms Inventory towards myself.

There's no time to waste and lots of work to do. So, let's get to it. We are going to do the dreaded and infamous 4th Step (of the 12-Step Program).

Personal Inventory

We are going to make another list. Yes, I know that you just burned the first one, and that is alright. This is because we do this practice many times in our life, because each time we do, we get to drill down into deeper layers of the same 'sin'.

On your list, make the following column headings:

Resentment/Anger
Fear
Selfishness
Dishonesty
Shame/Guilt
False Pride
Jealousy/Envy
MY JUDGMENT
MY PART

Then, as rows, list the people who you have had some form of conflict with (even if it was only internalized, like judgments or resentments). Leave plenty of room under each person. Excel or Microsoft tables work well for this, since you can expand them.

Start with one person, and go through every memory about your relationship and negative interactions with them.

After a thorough and honest assessment, checkmark the box of the emotion(s) you experienced for each memory. In the JUDGMENT column, write from your inner, shallow voice, what judgments you have held. What are your justifications for judging them, now or from the past.

In the final column, examine closely from the deeper, authentic voice, and answer the question, "What part did I play in this? What do I own?"

Feel free to expand as you need to. When I have done this each time, I end up with a short novel, to be thorough. Don't shy away from this practice. Dig into every emotional memory with every person and spew it out. Putting it onto paper makes it real and tangible and something you can work with.

Now, the next step with this practice is the next phase in our full Atonement. Once you've finished as completely as you can, contact a trusted friend. This can be anyone, so long as they can be trusted to hold what you are going to reveal in complete confidence and non-judgmentally. It works well with people who are familiar with 12-Step work, such as a counselor, a priest, a sponsor, etc.

If they aren't familiar, help them understand their role. It is not to offer you counseling or guidance, and it's certainly not to pity or fix you. Instead, they are to listen as you make your confession. As I spoke to in the Projection Practice, they are to simply hold space. They can ask clarifying questions so as to have you talk as deeply as possible, but they are mostly there to witness your taking ownership of everything on this list.

    For the final Step, go through EACH item and be witnessed by this friend.
    The miracle in the 4th Step is the release of frozen emotional tensions that we hold, that exist as long as we have these 'secrets.' When they are aired to a trusted friend, they instantly lose much of their power over you.
    You come clean. You confess. You own your part, and nothing more. Don't fall prey to owning more than your part, but don't fall short of owning every particle that belongs to you.
    Again, you get out of this what you put into it, so do it thoroughly and honestly.

    We are now getting very close to the bottom of the Inferno Pit. There is yet one more final stage to Atonement, before we meet the ultimate Demonic Angel. But, is that the final curtain call? I think not.
    And, although Virgil isn't allowing Dante any breaks, we have the luxury to do so. In fact, since we are doing inventory, it would be completely unfair to take stock of our liabilities alone, and not account for our assets too. So, I'm interrupting our pilgrimage of the Inferno, to include a small and deserved respite.
    The curtains close, and the theater lights brighten…..It's time for intermission.

Intermission

We are getting very close now, to the lowest and most vile Circles of Hell. We have only two more to progress until we meet the ultimate Archangel. And, before we progress any farther, it's time for an intermission of sorts. It's time to take stock of how far we've come. We traversed the downward spirals of Circles. We've looked into our thoughts, explored our emotions, met some of our Shadows, and started the healing of our inner and outer worlds. We've begun the arduous process of rebuilding relationships to our stories, emotive energies, thought patterns and habits. We've started new relationships with others, and all of our selves.

And yet, you might ask, what is left, is there more that I need to do? Isn't this meeting of penitent Shades over yet? Lest we forget, Beatrice is still waiting at the end of our pilgrimage, and we must continue, for our own full salvation and the beloved ultimate reunion. But first, we must do battle with the lowest of lethal creatures, and by the grace of the Gods, survive. Yes, we will continue the journey of our descent.

And, as was foretold in one of the oldest written tales of humankind, the Mesopotamian tale of Inanna, once we descend as low as the Underground takes us, where our very skin and muscle is torn from our bones and exposed for the filth that it is, we must still then make our way back out to the light. We must yet ascend. In Dante's world, we still need to fight our way back through Purgatorio, to meet Beatrice and find our way to the Heavenly God.

In my own journey, I recognized in myself that early on in my hajj I was so ravenous for more personal excavation that I couldn't get enough. I couldn't wait to meet my supreme tormentor and declare success and attainment. I was hell-bent to finish my recovery and rise from the ashes.

My intermission thus, didn't come from needing to stop and take a breath, nor to smell the roses. But come it did.

I had a wake-up call when I realized that not everyone else around me was in the same place as me. I was so 'high' on this new world of personal truth and integrity, I had lost perspective, and exactly how monumentally different my world was becoming.

To my utter surprise, I realized that the friends that I had had 'back then' were not as excited as I was to make a shift into personal empowerment. I was so sure that this 'high' would rub off on everyone around me and they would join me in this quest, but I found the Dark Forest very empty, quiet, and lonely.

No one from my past wanted to come with me through the Inferno. I couldn't fathom the idea that everyone didn't want the same thing as I did. It was a hard awakening, to acknowledge that I had changed and my many friends and family were no longer supportive friends and family.

It was a wise new friend who helped me understand that as my inner world was altering my outer world, everything else in my life would change too. Of course, this was the goal, but it does come with a price. In the end, the price is worth every bead of sweat, drop of blood, and every river of tears.

However, while I was so entrenched in my own personal work and shedding blood, sweat and tears, I had also forgotten to back-fill my cup. I had not celebrated along the way, I had not taken time for an intermission to take stock of how far I had come. In fact, I was behaving as though this was my new addiction.

I was depleted and nearing burn out, even though this was such powerfully filling work. No matter how fulfilling it was, it took a lot of energy to maintain the course, and stay plugged into the practices.

So, take some time for yourself throughout your journey, make a pitstop with every success. Always make the time to find your gratitude for having had the courage to make it this far. And find as many ways to do this as is possible.

Celebrate your journey so far!

Here are a few of my favorite ways to celebrate my accomplishments:

- **Ecstatic Dancing-** I love this! Put on some music to fit the mood you're in, and bring your awareness to your body. Be fully present in whatever way fits for you. Then, pay attention to the impulses you feel and follow them. Dance as though no one is watching, but you and the Universe. Make your dance a moving prayer of gratitude. Talk to the Universe in its language, that of emotion and feeling! Stir your energy up with bodily movement, and allow the energy of the Universe to fill you to overflowing. Dance out all that you've released, and dance in all of the freedom and liberation that replaces it.
- **Gratitude Jar** – Every day, find what you are most grateful for and write it down, making it real, and put it in your jar.
- **Meditate to YES!** – Follow your favorite method of meditation and enliven each cell in your body. Invite the energy of YES to each cell and feel the tingle of shakti, of life source. Open to <u>Receiving</u> the YES. Feel the invitation to YES in every cell, OPENING yourself fully to the unlimited possibilities of the Universe. She knows what work you've been doing, and that you are deserving. Watch out, once you do this, be prepared for anything to happen!
- **Join New Communities** – as we begin to learn how to relate in new ways, surround yourself with those who

are exploring new and more conscious ways to live too. You will find many, once you start to look. You will find that there are those you fit with and those you do not. Just know there is a tribe out there waiting for you. Find it and feel a new sense of belonging. Create and find your new Tribe!

- **Make an Asset Inventory** – we just made a liability inventory in the last practice. Reverse it, and list those experiences where you've done good things, where your assets have shown up, like love, compassion, service, forgiveness, honesty, trust, and humility. This can be even harder than the previous list, because we are taught not to shine our own light. But, shine you must, you deserve to!

Recognize how far you've come. Recognize the courage that it takes to undertake this journey in the first place. Recognize the progress you've made against all odds. And, always recognize how fortunate you are, to have had the life you've had, which is so full of potent opportunities for such sacred growth.

And, although I would like to tell you we're finished, I hear a waterfall, crashing in the distance......and eerily, and demandingly, it calls us back to Dante's world.

The curtains open and the lights are dimming.....

Dante and Virgil hear a waterfall as they exit the Circle of Violence. At the top of the falls, Virgil commands Dante to remove a cord from his waist and drop it over the edge. This is a call to Geryon, the Monster of Fraud, a dragon who has the tail of a scorpion, hairy arms, a painted serpentine body, wearing the face of an honest man.

Geryon allows Virgil and Dante to mount his serpentine back and Geryon takes flight. He circles slowly downward, against the upward blowing winds, descending to the rocks that are at the edge of the Eighth Circle, the Circle of Fraud.

"BEHOLD the monster with the pointed tail,
Who cleaves the hills, and breaketh walls and weapons,
Behold him who infecteth all the world."

The face was as the face of a just man,
Its semblance outwardly was so benign,
And of a serpent all the trunk beside.

Two paws it had, hairy unto the armpits;
The back, and breast, and both the sides it had
Depicted o'er with nooses and with shields.
Dante's Inferno, Canto XVII

Circle of Fraud

Of every malice that wins hate in Heaven,
Injury is the end; and all such end
Either by force or fraud afflicteth others.

But because fraud is man's peculiar vice,
More it displeases God; and so stand lowest
The fraudulent, and greater dole assails them.
Dante's Inferno, Canto XI

 Having arrived in this vast Circle, Virgil explains that Fraud, above all other sin, is the most vile according to the Divine Creator. For it is humans alone that can perpetrate various forms of fraud upon another. It requires some form of reasoning in order to betray, lie, and deceive. Thus, it is deliberate and intended. Of all of the animal kingdom, he is correct, we are the only creations on this planet that are capable of this harm.
 I might disagree that it is the lowest form of sin, but he does make a good point. In any case, we follow our devoted Dante into Malebolge, which means, the Evil Ditches in the Eighth Circle.
 This Circle is shaped like a large funnel of stone, like an amphitheater. Around the funnel run ten deep ditches where the tormented suffer. Each level holds its own brand of Fraud. For example, in Ditch Four, the Sorcerers are found. They will spend eternity with their heads twisted backward on their body, as retribution for their prying into the future of others, thus they will never again be able to look forward.
 In Ditch Three, the Simoniacs are found who sold ecclesiastic favors for money. The priestly sinners are placed head-downwards in baptismal fonts, with flames burning the soles of their eternally jerking feet.

Another interesting one I thought, was Ditch Two, where the Flatterers are steeped in all forms of filth and human excrement, as were their words in life.

Rather than visiting each Ditch though we can summarize Fraud as being willfully deceitful against another. The degree of intention involved and whether or not the deceit is direct or indirect not only has consequences in Dante's Hell, it does in other moral landscapes as well. For example, according to Rabbinic Judaism, the severity of the sinner's transgression, must be absolved with atonement. This atonement is dictated by an ordained court and the Torah. In addition to a minimum of repentance, atonement may also involve Yom Kippur services, restitution, lashing, or even death by stoning, strangulation, or burning.

In *A Course of Miracles (ACIM)*, which is a 1976 book by Helen Schucman thought to be channeled from Jesus to her directly, which has sold millions of copies and studied by many new-age Christianity groups and Christian mystics, has its base in atonement. In ACIM principles, atonement is not the ultimate path to peace, it is the peace itself. The ACIM does not mandate any earthly punishments for our transgressions at all. In fact, it states that we make no transgressions at all, as there is no sin, as we are all one and part of God itself. Total forgiveness of others and self leads to atonement.

Although I appreciate the diverse and extreme perspectives of these two philosophies, in my humanness, I looked for something between these two measures, something more in the middle, but just as meaningful. Deceitful sin is perpetrated through our words and action. Thus, it was with my words and action that I wished to make Atonement.

Words are powerful measures, no matter what language you speak. Again, humans above all other creatures on this lovely Planet, are blessed with this gift. And when we use our gift to willfully violate others to the extent that we create a fraudulent reality, we have committed the greatest of sin against others and the Divine.

Consider just how hurtful someone's words can be. They can absolutely destroy another. Combine them with willful deceit and action, and even the strongest of us will fall prey to heartbreak.

Words can also be the greatest of healers. They work especially well when accompanied by action and we'll do both here.

We are going to do Step 9 of the 12-Step Program, which reads,

Made direct amends to such people wherever possible, except when to do so would injure them or others.

Atonement of and by the Word

Making an apology and making an amend are two different things. An apology is part of making an amend, but not all. Making amends first and foremost, must be sincere. You must know what part you played without any excuse or story. Simply own exactly what you did wrong, and make tangible retribution.

You must also understand how your words or your actions affected the other. This is the cultivation of empathy, understanding, and the willingness to understand others' lives. We may or may not be right as to how someone else sees the world, but we can be willing to try and be open to new views.

Direct amends are the best to make, and they should be put into perspective to the extent of the damage we created. Direct means actually meeting with others to make our amends by speaking to what our part was, a in a direct confession, but it isn't the only way.

Indirect amends can be made through actions when direct amends can't be made (maybe someone has passed on, moved, or we don't know where they are), or when direct amends would cause further injury. An example of this might be where making the amend will deepen the hurt or bring other innocent parties in, rather than making clean retribution. In this case, a Living Amend would be better.

Another method of Indirect amends, are doing them in conjunction with Direct amends. For example, when trust has been severely damaged, the other party will hear your words, but if you back it up by 1) not doing it again and 2) making reparations, trust could be re-earned. For example, if you have stolen from someone, certainly a Direct amend is necessary, but you also must repay what you took.

You could go so far as to devote some time to a homeless shelter, and make it known that you are dedicating your service to a harmed party. This is another example of a Living Amend and is very powerful on the Karmic Scorecard.

One last important item to note, is that you aren't looking for absolution or forgiveness as your goal. In my experience, there are people on my list who won't give it no matter what. But, that didn't stop me from making them. And, I have found in many cases, what I made an amend for even came as a surprise to the other; they didn't even remember the transgression I had felt so guilty about for years.

Or, those that an amend was made to, who held such animosity that they didn't even recognize the amend for what it was. It matters not how others receive it, or if they in turn own their part, only that I did my best to make the amend as authentically, sincerely, and truthfully as possible.

Look at the 4th Step Personal Inventory in the previous chapter. Make as many of those amends to the people who you've named there. That means, in some form, communicate, act, and own what harm you have perpetrated upon their wellbeing. Speak to how you have brought harm, fully apologize for your part, and don't own their part. Only your own, but do so from the depths of your soul. Then regardless of how this lands in them, be done.

Your Atonement is as complete as it can be. You have only to learn now, and do your best to not make the same violations. And, we're human, so we will invariably need to continue this process of inventory keeping and atonement. You will get more comfortable with this with a little practice. And practice you will, for life will afford each us of ample opportunities for forgiveness, apology, amends, and atonement.

And now, we finally approach the Central Well, the Ninth and final Circle of Hell. Here, we will meet the ultimate Demon, our Fallen Angel. We have come far, cultivating the skills and weaponry that will be needed to survive this depth. We have met each Circle with courage, and not run from the Shades and terrors. We've faced each and endured to traverse yet the next.

Do not lose your nerve now, we've come so far. Actually, at this point, there is no alternative, turning back isn't an option since we're too far in. Staying still isn't an option, as we are still mortal like Dante, and not allowed to remain. Going forward can only mean one option, either life or death.

    Huge Giants stand in perpetual guard inside the Well with their legs embedded in the rocks and ice. Each Giant's torso and arms are chained, save one Giant.
    The Giant Antaeus was not chained as the others. Antaeus, during life, had performed one act of grace on behalf of the Gods, amongst his many other deeds of forbidden sin. And in return, his eternal condemnation held this small pardon.
    Virgil pleads with Antaeus to lower them into the deep well, and as Antaeus did in life, he gracefully takes them into his immense hands and lowers them into the Well, into Hell proper.

Yet in the abyss,
That Lucifer with Judas low ingulfs,
Lightly he placed us.

Canto XXXI., lines 133—135.

Circle of Treachery: Hell

When we were down within the darksome well,
Beneath the giant's feet, but lower far,
And I was scanning still the lofty wall,

Heard it said to me: "Look how thou steppest,
Take heed thou do not trample with thy feet
The heads of the tired, miserable brothers!"

Whereat I turned me round, and saw before me
And underfoot a lake, that from the frost
The semblance had of glass, and not of water

Livid, as far down as where shame appears,
Were the disconsolate shades within the ice,
Setting their teeth unto the note of storks.

Each one his countenance held downward bent:
From mouth the cold, from eyes the doeful heart
Among them witness of itself procures.

Dante's Inferno, Canto 32

Unlike all Hells ever described before and since, Dante's Hell is not a fiery netherworld. It was a frozen lake, the Lake of Cocytus. The freezing winds blow incessantly. Dante is cautioned by Virgil to watch his step crossing the ice as they will find the damned souls, sunken into the icy surface according to the degree of their sentence. Some Shades are completely contorted under the surface, others only with some degree of bodily exposure. All are frozen in eternal time, petrified in their icy damnation. Those with heads exposed downwardly face the ice staring at their own reflective fate in the glassy surface, their tears freezing their eyes open.

When first I read this, I was taken back by the lack of fiery damnation, which Dante has turned into an icy Hell instead. This very much brought to my mind the imagery of my teacher, Chameli Ardagh, when she speaks of all of our frozen emotion and stories within our psyches.

Another meaningful and unexpected twist is how gentle Antaeus the Giant was when transporting them into Hell. I expected something much more aggressive and violent. However, during my own journey to the lowest Hell, I came to understand the significance of this passage. I believe that by the end of our journey, you will understand it too.

This is the Circle of Treachery and the punished sinners are guilty of treason against those with whom they had special relationships and their God(s). Their treachery was denying love and all human warmth to those whom they could have loved, thus they are condemned to the icy Cocytus as their eternal destiny. They are the furthest removed from the light and warmth of the Sun. And deeper yet, in the center of the Cocytus, Lucifer awaits.

In this realm, we too will venture to the deepest parts of our being. It is time, my friends, to meet our Archangel, the one who began as the fairest of all angels. Who, by his own treachery of all that is Divine, is forever damned to be a giant, terrifying beast, frozen into the lake for all eternity.

Lucifer has three faces, each a different color. He has six wings which once were a beautiful and heavenly pearly white, are now dark, bat-like, and futile. Their eternal beating is the source of the icy wind which ensures Lucifer's eternal icy imprisonment, also holding all of the Treacherous Shades in the hoar frost.

Lucifer forever weeps from his six eyes, and his crystalline tears mix with bloody froth and pus as they stream down his three frothy chins. Each face has a giant mouth that gnaws eternally on prominent traitors, specially chosen by the Gods for this ultimate penitence. One of the traitors, is Judas the apostle who betrayed Christ.

Judas's felonious head is to be gnawed by Lucifer's yellowish fangs, screaming into Lucifer's salivating mouth for all of time. His splayed back is to be eternally flayed and shredded by Lucifer's mighty claws as the ultimate punishment that cannot ever be forgiven.

When we consider the deepest scar or wound within our souls or psyche, our imagination surely matches the vividness of Dante's description of Lucifer. What we venture to meet must be the vilest, most horrific of all demons. It has surely sabotaged everything we know of as a good life. It has brought crippling pain to our inner world, and overflowed to infect our outer world. It surely is an age-old wound, festering evermore, eternally afflicting our lives. Our suffrage and torment must be the fault of this supreme fiend.

Why would we even want to meet this being?

We've come so far already. But it is much more than that. We have already paved the way to this meeting with as much preparation as we can. The practices we have experienced thus far give us all the armor and shields we will need to meet the deepest parts of our self. We are ready to do battle with our ultimate Fate.

The practice of this Circle is going to integrate many of the teachings from the multitude of wisdom schools I've introduced. And they all came together for me recently, by themselves when I needed them the most. They simply merged in such a powerful way, and led me to a place I'd never dreamed of going. This mysterious melding was the gentle hand of Antaeus delivering me to the birthplace of my deepest Shadows lying under all that I knew.

Although gently, to Hell he did in fact, deliver me. I was delivered into a succession of Dark Nights of the Soul...and I survived.

The primary key here is not to rush to escape, but give yourself all the time that is needed for the darkest of Demons to appear. A small lifeline for you is that until you are truly prepared, these Demons- the vilest of all being Lucifer- will not appear before you are ready. Trust the process of your own evolution. Trust Virgil.

The process I underwent required a lot of capacity to follow the flows of my own evolutionary pilgrimage with trust and faith. You must be able to allow them to unfold as they will, with curiosity, and without the slightest hint of judgment or resistance.

You must be able to feel the nuanced shifts in energy and be able to follow these currents of unfolding. These flows are the inner linkages that allow you to descend deep enough to witness the very birthing of that which you fear the most. This practice is not intended to unfold in one session. Stay patient and, although it may feel like an eternity, where your being is gnawed and flayed by the demon forevermore, trust that it will unfold. If you've practiced with sincere honesty the techniques I've provided thus far, you're ready.

We will bring together our practices that we've learned. We will integrate our guides and imagery we've learned from the Shamanic traditions. We will meld the science of the Alpha/Theta state of our brain. We will draw from the wisdom of the ages knowing that we cannot resolve the problem from the place of the problem. We are immersed in the West Lodge of the Medicine Wheel where introspection is a Dark Cave full of possibility. We will ride the emotional tides that serve as portals to depths unknown, under all egoic thought and pattern. We will converse with our many Shadows as they tell of a Truth that is denied by our rational thought. We will welcome into our house, all of Rumi's guests. We will walk with the Watcher, right into the belly of Tolle's pain-body.

The key to this practice is flow. We'll need to be able to stay connected to the flows, the emotional flow and the flow of memory at the same time. And at the appropriate time, enter the realm of the Presence of the Watcher. It is through the eyes of the Watcher that we can remain conscious at this deepest level, within our unconscious flowing depths.

The integration with the deepest states of our mind, while maintaining access to Universal energy will allow us safe passage into the courage we will need to muster in order to continue to ask our self, "Is there yet another depth that I can descend into?"

We will certainly meet many beasts along the way, all armed with their own reasoning to not undertake the journey any farther. They will try to dissuade us from the Pit, giving us false counsel and dire warnings of deathly consequence. These we will recognize because we have already met them. We will know the most familiar; we have even given them names. But, there are those that still may lurk in the darkness and try to disrupt our descent. They may arise from the ice that entombs the Fraudsters desperate to keep us from the innermost Circle of the Lake of Cocytus.

We will have lists of reasons to convince us that we are not worthy of this final leg of the journey, displaying the Violence of our past. We may be met by the memories of those who withhold forgiveness from us. We may meet even our own inability to forgive ourselves.

Yes, there are many reasons not to undertake the final journey, to survive our Dark Night of the Soul. And yet….

There is the gentle hand of the Giant who delivers us here.

Dark Night of the Soul

The goal of this practice cannot be written by a 14th Century Poet, much less by me. It is only you who will unveil the eventual destination. Trust that it will be Divinely scripted.

I recommend reading through this practice, as we've done previously. Once you have a vague understanding of the flow, you might consider recording the practice in your own voice. I've provided a recording for you as well.

We will start with a request to descend as deeply as we are able, into the depths of the most core Shadow(s), to its very birthplace. And, because we may have more than one core Shadow, we may do this many times. Please don't try to do them all at once; you will have too many different 'flows' happening to be able to follow any one to its birthplace. So we will take this slowly, and choose one flow each time we practice.

Why do this at all?

At this stage in our journey, we have opened the gates and dialogued with and released many Shadows. But questions remained for me, "Where did they come from"? "Why are they even present in my life?" The Shadows may have answered these questions during our conversations, but I needed to know the 'how' that they were even requested to be created in the first place. I wanted to visit the very origin within me of their birthplace.

Understand that the asking of "Why," is yet another paradox and one that comes with a hint of caution. That is, that we can get stuck in the 'why' eternally, we can become frozen into the ice of Lake Cocytus.

However, it is in the mere asking of the question, that is the most powerful Universal ally. Stay in the fire of the question.

This is the ultimate quest and yields the greatest heat. So, this adventurous curiosity is the mindset that we will begin with.

Without further ado, to the core we go.

- Prepare yourself, with an environment and time to allow yourself safety, comfort, and freedom from the outside world.
- Settle in and get comfortable. Kleenex box at your disposal.
- Do the Induction Meditation or whatever practice that brings you deeply into a relaxed, meditative state of mind.
- Frame for yourself the question, "I wish to witness the birth of my Shadow of _____." Choose a Shadow that comes from the very Valley of Desolation. Feel the power in this Shadow, and the strength and presence of the Watcher asking this specific question. Separate the strong, intentional request of the Watcher, from the desperation of the 'need to know' or the ego-fear which may come from the Shadow itself fearing exposure.
- As with Shamanic Journeying, begin by repeating your request three times, clearly, and engage your imagination to take you to your Launch Pad, that place in nature where you feel most safe and protected.
- Feel the request and call to your Shadow.
- Wait patiently, and watch for the Shadow to appear.
- Allow yourself to fully BECOME the energy of the Shadow. Feed this energy. Grow this energy, to as large as you can, and hold onto it.
- Now...engaging your memory...remember...go back in time when you first felt this energy, as early as you can.

(FOLLOW the EMOTION only- RIDE IT. Do not judge anything that shows up).
- Once you've arrived at the earliest time you can identify, ask yourself as many times as you need, "Is there something under this?" (you are looking for the base, core emotion or experience, and this may yet lead you deeper, to another experience with another emotion- follow the flow as far as you can).
- Once you've gotten as deep as you can go, bring this earliest time into your memory. <u>Experience</u> this time again...fully.
- Expand your experiential memory, by expressing in movement, or sound, or however this experience is asking you to express it. And flow with the expression as it wants and needs to flow, for as long as you can- here you ride again, and the longer you ride, the more you will get.
- Now....be still, breathe.......Become the Watcher and watch.......(Again, lots of time needs to be allowed here, to allow for the unfolding of whatever occurs, emotionally, visually, however it unfolds).
- As a loving adult, step into the picture...(Flow with what happens as your adult self enters the event. Here we trust our connection to the evolutionary energy of Love, and that what needs to happen right now, will).
- When you are ready, bring your awareness back to your body, in this room......... breathe deeply.
- As the Watcher, journal.

Although it's only taken you 1-2 minutes to read through this, allow yourself ample time for riding the emotion back in time, and to get underneath what you thought might have been there. Then you need ample time to re-experience wherever you find yourself. You want to allow yourself to sink as deeply as you can, and this takes time, as well as huge courage and the greatest of perseverance.

You may find that for whatever reason, you don't feel you've gotten to the very bottom. This is absolutely alright as this is a very advanced practice. But don't let that stop you from doing the exact same practice again in the future. The amazing thing is that once you've traveled down the path with this Shadow, the next time you practice with this same Shadow, you can retrace your path much more easily. That is, if it was the right path to begin with. Feel your way cautiously, curiously, and DISCERN if this still feels like the right path back in emotional memory.

I know this may seem confusing, and there is little consolation I can give you. Much of what happens is strictly between you and Your Higher Power. Staying with the Shadow's raw emotion to earlier and earlier times brings you hopefully, to the earliest time. Keep asking if it is the earliest and expect the unexpected. Ride what comes. Then, experience the birthplace of your Shadow, as yourself, then as the Watcher and your loving adult.

And, more than anything, let your own experience unfold as it is supposed to for you.

The basic premise can be summarized this way:

1. Connect with the <u>emotion</u> of your Shadow
2. Follow it to earlier times when it showed up- to the earliest possible
3. Dig under the emotional layer- is there anything deeper? Ride the flow of emotion
4. Re-experience as you were back then and release it
5. Engage the Watcher, then send in your loving adult

Maybe an example would help.

Maggie's Dark Night of the Soul *(One of many I might add)*

Of the many fears that I've carried in my lifetime, I have always experienced this fear of losing relationships. I intentionally chose this for one of my earliest practices as it seemed very charged and strong for me. There are many 'ideas' that I have about this, but the raw emotion is one of desperate fear. Of course, any psychological textbook will diagnosis it as a fear of abandonment. But, that didn't fit with my reality.

My childhood was not filled with what a lot of others were. My parents didn't divorce, didn't fight, weren't abusive, and were what every child could hope for. My family was perfectly supportive, loving, and seemed highly functional. So, where did this fear come from? How had I taken it into my life and become so self-abusive that I turned to alcoholism as an escape route? Where had I been so lethally wounded, received my core wounds that I had been ready to destroy my life?

I could see certain tenets, but nothing was clear. In one way, my fear of loss had manifested itself throughout my life as enraged jealousy and a deep distrust for men. But again, my father was a veritable milk-toast. The closest he ever came to being a letch was the girly calendar he kept in the garage, which had a plastic film bikini on it, so when you lifted the plastic you saw a 1950's version of a naked pin-up girl. As 6 year-olds, we thought that was really something, sneaking into the garage to lift the plastic. But certainly no wounding there.

In preparing for my practice with great curiosity, I wrote about experiencing enraged jealousy. I journaled about a dream that I had had, that stirred this same emotion:

At the party, Peter is talking to a beautiful woman in red across the room. He catches me watching him and I can see him laugh at me dismissively, because he doesn't care and is moving on with someone better.

I am nothing...I am dismissed...I am not enough. I feel enraged.

My request then was, I wish to witness the birthplace of my Shadow of Enraged Jealousy.

I have a meditation and practice room I've prepared in my house that I use whenever I practice. I settled in, lit some incense, and played some very soft music. And, I used my version of the Induction Practice to begin my journey. I visited my Launch Pad, which is a clearing, deep in the forest with a fire burning in the center of a Medicine Wheel.

I began by remembering the dream of Peter and the woman in the red dress.

Then, I detached from the 'story,' the party room, Peter and the beautiful woman in red. All that remained was the raw emotion. I began to focus on the emotion, making it as big and all-encompassing as I could.

I felt the raw emotional surge and it took me, swept me away, making me wonder if I could actually live through it...I stayed in the fire of the emotion, no matter what. It felt like a righteous anger mixed up with sadness and life-threatening fear. I kept following the unique mix of toxic emotions, to earlier times when I had felt the same mix.....the emotional chain-link back in time.

It took me to earlier and earlier times when I had felt this same wave of initial anger, but whose deeper emotion I discovered was really a nauseating desperate fear. Then, I followed that fear.

I rode the emotion into memories of childhood, where I feared being in groups of playing children, because I didn't think they liked me because I wasn't fun. I could hear them laugh at me too, like Peter had. I felt the dismissal because I didn't know how to play right. I saw memories flash of being ashamed because my Barbie doll was an imitation Barbie and not the real thing. I feel ashamed in front of my best friend, Lesa. I followed that shame.

I kept going...but each earlier memory didn't FEEL like the original yet, there was nothing yet like a 'birthplace,' and certainly nothing as potent as I had felt as an adult. I asked to go deeper.

I saw myself in the crib, and maybe this was real, maybe not. But I followed the emotional memory anyhow to a night where I felt that no one would come back, and I cried and cried for someone to return. I could feel the 'dismissal,' and the fear tied to that. But, I knew it wasn't the core yet. I felt- no sensed- the dismissal from Mom, not Dad. This begged the question, "Where did the male part of this journey come from then"?

I forced myself to dismiss the confusion which could have caught me up in its deceptive web, and kept following the emotional memory and feelings of dismal. It led to darkness, to a still nothingness.

I felt confused as to where I was. It didn't matter, because I was touching the same toxic mix of emotion that I experience as an adult, and it was fierce in its strength. It seemed to be all of me, I was all-consumed by it. I felt (knew) that I had found my Lucifer. But, where was I, what was happening, I could not tell.

Without my calling her in, my Watcher became present in that moment and everything became crystal clear in an instant.

This toxic, emotional mix was not mine.

It belonged to someone else, someone very close in this moment, but running through my body too. It was my own Mother's emotions flowing through me; I was yet to be born.

My Watcher saw the replay of her life prior to meeting and marrying my father less than a year before my conception.

She had been severely abused by two bastard husbands, even to the extent that it had cost the life of one of the three children she had had. Her fear was very real, I could smell it, I could taste it. I felt her protective bear energy, as she was the only one who could protect her children as they were lethally threatened by these men. The energy of dismissal had been ever-present as she never felt she mattered. The desperation was a response to the need to hold onto a better man, my Father, who had surely been the first gentle and loving man she had ever known. Her Virgil, her Antaeus.

Her own mother had lived through several abusive and womanizing husbands, so my mother's childhood hadn't even held a 'fatherly' male. It was generationally thick, this patriarchal abuse. I could sense the thickness of the ice, the eternal grip she was caught in, and the desperation to feel the security that she had finally found in my father.

So, my conception being only 30 days after her marriage to my Father, was surely during a period of disbelief and deep doubt as to her worthiness to hang onto him, and desperation to do so. And, the desperation, hurt, doubt, distrust, and disbelief felt as thick as cold molasses. In fact, the emotions felt so old and hardened, like turning the molasses into fossilized amber.

But, in the moment of my discovery of this maternal Hell, I felt the hardened amber dissolve into warm honey, and it flowed, and flowed. As did my tears...

The frozen, hardened emotion, turned into warm liquid...and it flowed. Maybe for the first time in generations. It seemed to flow for many women in my lineage. It flowed for a very long time. As the flow began to ease, my Watcher called in my Midwife.

In the moment of birth of my emotional mix, Maggie, my Midwife, simply sat and held me and my pregnant Mother. She held us both in her loving, ample, and understanding lap.

It was in that moment that I understood the gentleness of the Giant's hand. More importantly, I understood that what I had envisioned as my Lucifer, had been birthed as an Angelic Protector. She was, in my case, actually birthed long ago, by another woman, maybe many generations ago. The unique mix that included the desperation component, was a fairly new derivation that my Mother created, for her own protection.

In loving memory of my Mother who has since passed and walked the Rainbow Bridge, let me say that after she married my Father, she evolved into the most dynamic woman I have ever met. She found her own inner strength, and accomplished more with less than anyone I know. She jumped from airplanes, created and published her own magazine (without even a high school education), she taught herself to ranch, farm, flew planes, and built houses. She didn't carry her desperation and fear along with her through the remainder of her life. She did anything she wanted, and I can only wish the same strength to women today, as we all wake up from a very long period of dismissal and desperation. What was her Dark Night of the Soul like, and how did she do this? I'll never know, as we never got a chance to talk about this. But respect her immensely, I do. And, I told her so on her deathbed.

As with any Shadow, they are all birthed in moments where the innocence of our humanness and something we love is lethally threatened by something. They are birthed to help protect us either physically, psychically, emotionally, energetically, or mentally. They were Heavenly Angels at first with the same brilliant pearly white wings that Lucifer once possessed.

It was my own treachery born of desperate fear that had caused the fall from grace. I had frozen the Lake of Cocytus with the beating of my own egoic wings. I had created my own Fallen Angel, my own Lucifer, innocently, albeit as toxic as the waters of the River Phlegathon. Ultimately though, in being willing to venture to my own Hell, many years later, the ice had finally started to thaw.

Let's go back to Dante's Hell.....

Dante and Virgil meet Lucifer. Dante, who is so fearful he cannot write, describes his meeting:

I did not die, and I alive remained not;
Think for thyself now, hast thou aught of wit,
What I became, being of both deprived.
                                               Dante's Inferno, Canto XXXIV

Virgil leads them closer, they can smell the breath of the Devil himself. They can sense the everlasting agony of his gnawing fangs and ripping claws and the sheer magnitude of Lucifer's immense anguish and daunting power. And then, something incredible happens.

Nothing

Virgil awaits the right moment to escape, where all of Lucifer's wings are raised high, and jumps onto Lucifer's hairy body with Dante hanging onto his back. They scramble down his huge, hairy body and when they get to his genitalia, they turn around, and scramble backward.

In this world of the Otherworldly, somehow this turns the world upside down, and they are exiting Hell by climbing backward down Lucifer's legs into a tunnel where the morning awaits them.

Why was Dante's eventual and arduous journey to meet Lucifer finished without any hell-bending, diabolical discourse or horrific episode befitting such a lavishly horrid tale?

Because, ours doesn't either. We too, can turn our worlds around and find the morning sun at the end of our Dark Night of the Soul.

We have finished our descent to the darkest of places in our soul. Is this where the story ends? It cannot, because we must Ascend yet or live forever here.

Purgatorio

*Sweet colour of the oriental sapphire,
That was upgathered in the cloudless aspect
Of the pure air, as far as the first circle,*

*Unto mine eyes did recommence delight
Soon as I issued forth from the dead air,
Which had with sadness filled mine eyes and breast.*

*The beauteous planet, that to love incites,
Was making all the orient to laugh,
Veiling the Fishes that were in her escort.*
                              Dante's Purgatrio, Canto I

Dante and Virgil emerge from the Inferno, to discover that it is a dawn of a new day…..early, Easter morning. He sees the constellation Pisces rising into the dawning sky.

In contrast to the deathly boatman Charon in the Inferno, they are given passage across the sea by an Angel Boatman to the shores of the Mountain of Purgatory this Easter morning. This is the place where souls are converted from the sorrow and misery of sin, into a state of Grace preparing them for entrance into Paradise.

Dante's first night before scaling the Terraces of Purgatory, he falls asleep and dreams.

In dreams it seemed to me I saw suspended
An eagle in the sky, with plumes of gold,
With wings wide open, and intent to stoop,
………
Then wheeling somewhat more, it seemed to me,
Terrible as the lightning he descended,
And snatched me upward even to the fire.

Therein it seemed that he and I were burning,
And the imagined fire did scorch me so,
That of necessity my sleep was broken.
Dante's Purgatorio, Canto IX

Dante dreams that he is swept up by an Eagle, who flies as high as the fire of the Sun. He awakens to find himself at the gate of Purgatorio, Peter's Gate. They climb the three steps to the gate, and are met by an Angel.

Along the three stairs upward with good will
Did my Conductor draw me, saying:
"Ask Humbly that he the fastening may undo."

Devoutly at the holy feet I cast me,
For mercy's sake besought that he would open,
But first upon my breast three times I smote.

Seven P's upon my forehead he described
With the sword's point, and, "Take heed that thou wash
These wounds, when thou shalt be within," he said.

Ashes, or earth that dry is excavated,
Of the same colour were with his attire,
And from beneath it he drew forth two keys.

One was of gold, and the other was of silver;
First with the white, and after with the yellow,
Plied he the door, so that I was content.

"Whenever faileth either of these keys
So that it turn not rightly in the lock,"
He said to us, "this entrance doth not open.

Dante's Purgatorio, Canto IX

The Guardian Angel has carved seven "P"'s into Dante's forehead with the tip of his mighty sword gleaming in the morning's first light. The P's stand for Peccatum, a Latin word which refers to 'sin', and seven times representing the seven cardinal sins.

Futher, he provides us thus, the means for which to navigate Purgatory in his proclamation to Dante. The Mountain of Purgatory is encircled with seven Terraces, each offering souls the chance to learn from past mistakes and cleanse themselves. Once a soul is cleansed at each Terrace, then one "P" will be removed by the Angel granting passage to the next terrace.

The Angel holds two keys, one gold and one silver. If the keys open the door for those who request entrance, they are allowed to continue their journey.

Unlike Dante, we aren't going to have to traverse each of the seven Terraces, to earn the erasing of, or baptism from, the carved "P"'s. However, these Terraces are as fabulous as the Circles of the Inferno and definitely worth a full read. But for now, we will circumvent just a bit.

Part of any age-old mythological journey is the Hero's return after having met his incredulous challenges and slain the beast. It is also commonly known as the Hero's or Heroine's Journey, where the Hero must Descend and conquer, then Ascend into victory and triumph. In Dante's pilgrimage, Purgatorio is where we would find ourselves in between, in a process of cleansing first.

During my own journey, I also found that there was a reckoning period, after having met some of the initial and painful challenges, before I could find my Nirvana, enlightenment, Heaven, or Peace. I truly don't subscribe to the idea that once we've done all of our work, life is all Heaven and Gold. We continue to live in the same world with the same pressures and same challenges.

Before I could live from a different place, sourcing energy and thought from a cleaner inner landscape, I had to learn how to live from this new terrain. A reckoning was at hand for me.

It's easy to feel a glow when I'm practicing, in a seminar, class, workshop, or even by myself. However, how do I access this part of me once I step outside into the real world and I have to face traffic, pollution, ignorance, rude people, sudden crisis, or heartbreak? It seemed to me to be an elusive state, where I found peace, but only when things were peaceful. As with the souls on the Terraces, I will still face 'tests' to see if I can live integrally and walk my talk, if you will, whilst in the throes of real life.

We have undergone tremendous resurrection of our authenticity already. And, there is still more that we can do to prepare ourselves for our future. Just as Dante dreamed, Eagles are waiting to fly us towards the Sun. There are merciful Angels that we can call upon when we need a gate opened.

If we follow the Golden Thread from the many traditions that I've talked about, we are now deep into the Transformation stage. In this stage, we actually change, and our Shadows are transmuting. We aren't changing who we are at our core. We are changing what and how we choose...choosing to live, from our renewed core. We are changing what we resource within ourselves and outside of ourselves to thrive, rather than suffer. We choose, rather than unconsciously submit. And, we choose this change because we begin to love and trust who we are at our core.

> *WHEN we had crossed the threshhold of the door*
> *Which the perverted love of souls disuses,*
> *Because it makes the crooked way seem straight.*
> *Dante's Purgatorio, Canto X*

Purgatory, as explained by Virgil, our devoted guide, is a place of love. However, it was abused and misused by the penitent souls. Thus, they must remember what love actually is and where they can find it again.

Loving oneself is a transformation we must make before we can shower this onto others. Furthermore, trust in one's self needs to be harvested before we can be trusting in relationship with others, ourselves, and our world. We must trust ourselves to love, and love well. But love doesn't blossom by itself; it takes the union of love and trust to be strong enough to face our future challenges.

The Guardian Angel of the gate holds the keys, both the Gold of our Love, and the Silver of our Trust.

And, the Gate opened....

Virgil leads us through the gate into a new landscape.

Intuition

Inner trust of one's self can be nurtured through a deeper connection to and our love for our Intuition.

Virgil, who has guided us throughout, is like our intuition. He speaks from inside the landscape, sometimes with a warning, and sometimes with assurance. Another interesting thing about Virgil, much like our intuition, is that he is utterly unconditional. He is not motivated by fear, or even love, and he is completely non-judgmental. He was given one task by Beatrice; to guide Dante, and under no circumstances leave him.

Such is our intuition. It is intuition that can be cultivated to be our guide. In fact, it already is, it is just that we don't always listen to it. Even worse, we aren't trained to hear it.

Rumi said, *"There is a voice that doesn't use words. Listen."*

Intuition has its own language, and it is unique to each of us. We need to be willing however, to learn a new language. I, for one, don't hear it in words. It comes to me in a certain sensation in my body. And, I am still learning how to listen attentively.

What intuition actually is, no one really knows. There are hundreds of theories that suggest everything from subconscious complexes coming from the deep to inform us, to extra-terrestrial multi-dimensional information. I find some value in both the esoteric as well as scientific theory.

I have been a science buff from a very young age, and what I find fascinating in today's quantum sciences, is that science is starting to say what the sages have said all along. The Universe is 99.9999+% vibrational energy and that everything is connected at this level.

In Vedic scriptures, Aum is the primordial sound, the breath of Brahman which created the Universe. It is the language of vibration, bringing the unmanifest into manifestation.

According to Kabbalah mystics, the fundamental fabric of the cosmos is sound, the sound of each Otiyot, a Divine Letter. Each Otiyot is a varied articulation of creative energy that generates our material world. And that energy is in a state of perpetual oscillation. This is the exact thinking behind science's String Theory. Again, vibrational energy underlying everything in the Universe, source energy creating vibrational energy creating matter.

In the Christian Bible's Gospel of John, the birth of creation was the 'Word' of God, the Logos. And John defines the true identity of Jesus, who is the Word of God through whom the world was created and who took on human form. The Word being sound, or maybe the Higgs Boson or God Particle?

Another name for vibration is resonance. And, again in both science and spirituality, we find wonderous similarities across thousands of years and hundreds of languages. Science says that vibration organizes matter into complex forms repeatably, according to frequency. Nature shows us this with fantastic phenomena such as the Fibonacci Sequence that mathematically dictates a perfect spiral. We see it in the arms of galaxies, seashells, the flight pattern of hunting birds-of-prey, and weather patterns, amongst thousands of others.

Spiritually, the reverence for circles and spirals have found their way into every indigenous culture throughout time. And, these same types of geometric algorithms display themselves in fractal patterns, what spiritual sages have called Sacred Geometry for eons.

One of the most fascinating aspects of fractals is their inherent holographic nature, where each element is a perfect reflection of the whole. This is the fundamental principle in Buddhism as well, where each entity in the Universe is also a perfect reflection of the Universe. This idea can be referred to as 'integral unity.' The integral unity of the whole manifests itself in the parts, and they, in turn, aspire to unite with the whole.

Carl Sagan, a famous astrophysicist famously said, *"We are the Universe experiencing itself."*

Other very scientific minds have a deep appreciation for the esoteric as well, such as Einstein, and Nikola Tesla, discoverer of the electromagnetic force. Tesla explained, *"All perceptible matter comes from a primary substance, or tenuity beyond conception, filling all space, the akasha or luminiferous ether, which is acted upon by the life giving Prana or creative force, calling into existence, in never-ending cycles all things and phenomena."*

It's my belief that our intuition is a connection to this etheric field of energy, both being proven by quantum physics and taught by multiple spiritual traditions, which now merge into one another. Einstein conceded that he didn't understand intuition, but respected it highly as his connection to something beyond mind and logic.

Einstein said, *"The intuitive mind is a sacred gift."*

It actually matters not, what we believe intuition is. What matters is that it can be a very helpful tool when we are facing real life. It provides our inner ability to trust, and to discern. Discernment helps us achieve trust in our inner ability to know what is in our best interests, and what is not.

To tie it all together then, we can use our intuition to discern, through resonance, and build our foundation of self-trust, which nourishes our sustainable capacity of self-love.

Resonance is the feeling we get when we experience the synchronization of our own vibrational field to something that is pulsating the same as we. Think of two guitars on either side of a large room. When one guitar strikes a perfect G, the G string on the other guitar will vibrate as well. They are resonating with each other.

Similar to theories of the Law of Attraction, resonance works the same way. As the Law of Attraction states, "Like energy attracts like energy."

Our intuition picks up the vibrations from our world, and lets us know, through our body, whether something resonates for us or not. Does it oscillate or vibrate within the same frequencies that we exist within? Our ability to recognize this resonance within is the cultivation of intuition. And, as with any muscle, it strengthens with practice. There are several ways to do this.

You can start with experimenting with information that you know to be true, or false. Explore how it feels when you tell yourself something you know to be true. Then, explore how you feel when you tell yourself something you know is false.

Even better, how does it make you feel, to act with integrity, even in uncomfortable situations, versus how do you feel when you know you've acted outside your values? You can feel the difference. There is a resonance that will become evident in your body somehow, that you can learn to tune into. And this sensation will become familiar with awareness and practice, and becomes distinguishable from the words which is the language of the ego. This has been my key to learning which voice to listen to, and know the difference between ego and intuition.

But what about discerning between what I believe to be true, and what is actually true? Can intuition help here?

We've all heard that we need to learn to live more from our hearts than our heads. I too, find that very useful where I associate living from my heart to mean from emotional intellect and my head being associated with the crazy mental realm.

However, I looked at this dynamic as lacking something, and that something was Universal Truth. I needed to be able to pull into this dynamic the idea of Universal Intelligence, to help inform my humanness, and separate my truth from reality.

I didn't want to be run only on emotion, informing my mind and decision-making. This seemed like this meant I was subject to the movements of emotional energy. And vice versa, I didn't want my reasoning brain to inform my emotions alone, either.

Furthermore, this 'informing' from either in isolation, seemed to me to be where my journey started in the first place. Something was missing. And, it was the intuitive knowing that comes from a connection to Universal Truth (big "T"), that which is beyond my truth (little "t").

I learned a practice that helped me 'add' that ingredient to my everyday life, that I've come to Trust (big "T").

Three Realm Practice

In this practice, start with using questions that are simple, not complex. Build your way with practice to more complex questions. Additionally, with a little practice, you can use this same practice in your everyday life, when you need to access your intuition anywhere you find yourself. Begin by sitting, to make it easier to do successfully at first.

Simple questions might be:
"What do I want to do with my afternoon?"
"Should I ask her to lunch today?"

As you begin to build your ability to discern Truth from truth, your questions can grow to the biggies in life:
"Do I trust him?"
"What is my purpose?"
"Do I love myself?"

Imagine yourself with three realms.
    Mental – head space
    Heart – upper chest
    Belly – lower torso

1. Sitting quietly, ask yourself a question.
2. Bring your awareness to your Mental Realm, and ask that Realm the question. Listen for the answer, no matter how it arrives.
3. Bring your awareness to your Heart Realm, and do the same.
4. Finally, bring your awareness to your Belly Realm, and ask again. Listen closely for how the answer comes.

What I have found with this simple practice, is that there is a very clear delineation between the three answers. The key is to isolate the question and answer to one realm at a time, using your awareness. Don't let them 'leak' into each other.

Invariably, I get three very distinct and different responses. Yours may be different, but in my experience with others, they have generally agreed that the answers from the Mental Realm are based on logic, want, and ego. The sense of the answers that come from the Heart Realm are emotionally based, and more of the 'wants' we would prefer.

The one that is found generally to be the most integral, and Truthful (big "T") is the one received from my Belly Realm. It isn't always the answer wanted, but it seems to come more from a concerned, unbiased, and very wise friend. It can oftentimes be the answer that one would get using the principles of compassion and altruism. This can be extremely different than what "I want", or "me-centric" answer.

I have found that by using this simple method, especially when I am conflicted by logic and emotion, I can get perspective on differing options, answers, or possibilities.

My Belly Realm always feels more 'just' and balanced than the other two. That doesn't mean that they are 'wrong', but more isolated and unbalanced. When I can clearly hear the differences though, and inform decisions with these perspectives, I experience a feeling of "justness' or 'rightness' and a lack of doubt in an eventual and integral answer. I feel certain, clear, and accepting.

For me, I have taken this idea and integrated it into my life, so that I am actively engaging that 'something greater than I' into my everyday life. My Belly Realm seems to be that place that is the origin of my intuitive voice. I now 'inform' my daily life, from the bottom-up, rather than top-down and it serves me well.

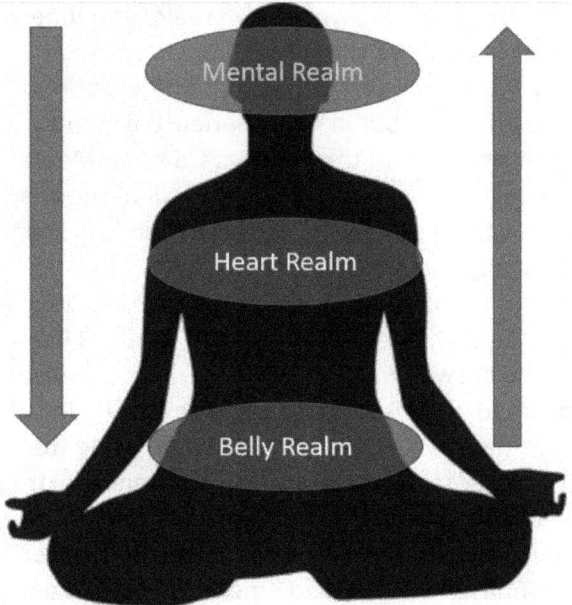

Which way do you inform?

    The cultivation of intuition and building inner Trust is the Silver Key that the Angel used to unlock the Gate. Let's look at the Golden Key.

Self Love

"Your job is to fill your own cup, so it overflows. Then, you can serve others from your saucer."
Lisa Nichols

It's so true. You've probably heard that we can't give what we don't have. In our world today, most of us are driven to utter exhaustion. From an empty well, we continue to try to fill the needs of others. So, when our well runs dry, then what?

And then of course, we have the planted idea that to love ourselves above others is selfish. It might be, but we aren't trying to love ourselves more than we love others. We are trying to find a source of fulfillment that allows our reservoir to naturally spill over onto everyone else around us.

It's especially difficult when we begin our awakening into our inner landscape, to not feel a sense of shame about what we have found in the process. None of us are saints, and to be able to forgive ourselves for any damnable sin can be hard. I've certainly struggled with that.

I learned however, what it means to feel love when I became a Mother. I believe it is the most powerful energy in the world, the love we have for our children. It is truly the supreme definition of unconditional love. My children could commit the most grievous of sins, and I would forgive them instantly. I might be angry, but forgiveness would be there unconditionally. If I'm totally honest, I can't say that I have this type of love for any other human.

It is this same type of unconditionality that I sought to find and give to myself. Forgiveness is the Golden Key.

For me, forgiveness came the day that I simply accepted that I was imperfectly perfect, as it says in the Course of Miracles. I couldn't sin, as sin doesn't actually exist at all. It veritably violates Divine Law.

I have certainly made a lot of mistakes in my years, and hurt many people along the way. This made me feel unforgivable at first. I simply accepted that yes, I was responsible for having caused those harms. And, then I became accountable to be a better person, learning from my transgressions, and making amends. This clears the slate as much as can be done. The rest, well, is letting go of it. I could fill my cup with the everlasting drip of poison, or I can move on past the regret.

This led me to a very deep, and somewhat new understanding of empathy, which is the ability to feel what another person is experiencing from within their frame of reference. That is, the capacity to place oneself in another's position. At a minimum, even if I don't have a full understanding of someone's landscape, I can be willing to accept that theirs is different than my own and of just as much importance.

Applying empathy then, means that I need to project the same level of forgiveness onto others that I do to myself. For me, it became the integral aspect of this extension that drew me to practice Ho'oponopono.

Historically, it is an ancient Hawaiian spiritual practice, that spread throughout the South Pacific many eons ago. It was initially used when a member of the tribe was making a public amend and the tribe forgave them. The early cultural beliefs of those tribes included a belief that we are all connected as one, so the pubic forgiveness extended to all other sentient beings, as a sin of one was a sin of all. The forgiveness of one, was a universal forgiveness of all. This was true altruism for me.

The Ho'oponopono can be used when forgiveness from another may or may not come, but we have made amends as best we can. It can allow us to 'let it go.' And, it is extremely useful for self-forgiveness, which by any measure is the most difficult of all to give and receive.

When I experienced the death of my first husband I used this practice to assuage deep feelings of guilt and remorse.

Ho'oponopono Practice

Used as a mantra, to be repeated until one feels into the meaning of the words. As with any prayer, it is the feeling, not the words that express in the language of the Universe.

Mantras are ritually repeated 108 times. They can be counted by using a Mala (108 beaded Hindu chain), Prayer

Beads, or a Rosary. If you don't have a way of keeping count, it doesn't matter as much as the intention to repeat the words until you fall deeply into them. You can set an alarm or better yet, play some music for a period of time and keep going until it ends.

Repeat these words as a Mantra or Prayer:

I'm sorry,
please forgive me,
thank you,
I love you.

With self-forgiveness, you can clear the path of any barriers you have to self-love. A maintenance program is necessary to keep your cup full. This is a non-negotiable!

In addition, give yourself special days, gifts, dinner out, an afternoon off, whatever you wish, to keep your cup full. It may take some folks longer than others to accept the self-given gifts, but I promise, you are deserving and worth every one. And the effort you take to show yourself love will pay the greatest dividends in your life.

Also, take care of your body, mind, and soul. Eat well, get plenty of sleep, meditate regularly, exercise, and make yourself a priority in your life.

"You yourself, as much as anybody in the entire universe, deserve your love and affection."
Buddha

And said: "The temporal fire and the eternal,
Son, thou hast seen, and to a place art come
Where of myself no farther I discern.

By intellect and art I here have brought thee;
Take thine own pleasure for thy guide henceforth;
Beyond the steep ways and the narrow art thou.

Behold the sun, that shines upon thy forehead;
Behold the grass, the flowerets, and the shrubs
Which of itself alone this land produces.

Until rejoicing come the beauteous eyes

Which weeping caused me to come unto thee,
Thou canst sit down, and thou canst walk among them.

Expect no more or word or sign from me;
Free and upright and sound is thy free-will,
And error were it not to do its bidding;

Thee o'er thyself I therefore crown and mitre!"
                              Dane's Purgatorio, Canto XXVII

    Virgil, who has faithfully guided Dante thus far is ready to take his leave. He bids Dante a loving farewell. He promises that Dante's love, Beatrice, will come to him soon.
    He praises Dante for his attainment of free-will, and reminds him to 'do its bidding.' Virgil honors Dante and his transformation of "thee, over thyself."

    I too, honor you, your courage, and transformation! I bow….

Paradise

Now since the universal atmosphere
Turns in a circuit with the primal motion
Unless the circle is broken on some side,

Upon this height, that all is disengaged
In living ether, doth this motion strike
And make the forest sound, for it is dense;

And so much power the stricken plant possesses
That with its virtue it impregns the air,
And this, revolving, scatters it around;

And yonder earth, according as 'tis worthy
In self or in its clime, conceives and bears
Of divers qualities the divers trees;

It should not seem a marvel then on earth,
This being heard, whenever any plant
Without seed manifest there taketh root.

And thou must know, this holy table-land
In which thou art is full of every seed,
And fruit has in it never gathered there.
      Dante's Purgatorio, Canto XXVIII

    As Dante enters the Earthly Paradise, he expresses how like Eden this must be. In the forest, he looks for his Beatrice, but first meets a beautiful woman, named Matilda, who is much like the proverbial Eve. She explains at length the self-generating and miraculous nature of the macrocosm and eco-system. And as they approach the River Lethe, Dante finally sees his long-lost love.

*Over her snow-white veil with olive cinct
Appeared a lady under a green mantle,
Vested in colour of the living flame.*

*And my own spirit, that already now
So long a time had been, that in her presence
Trembling with awe it had not stood abashed,*

*I saw the Lady, who erewhile appeared
Veiled underneath the angelic festival,
Direct her eyes to me across the river.*

*Although the veil, that from her head descended,
Encircled with the foliage of Minerva,
Did not permit her to appear distinctly,*

In attitude still royally majestic
Continued she, like unto one who speaks,
And keeps his warmest utterance in reserve:

"Look at me well; in sooth I'm Beatrice!
                            Dante's Purgatorio, Canto XXX

Dante sees Beatrice, and describes her with many Divinely enchanting attributes. One of the most notable, is that he says she is wearing a veil encircled with foliage, like the Crown of Minerva. Minerva was the ancient Grecian Goddess of Wisdom. He is so taken by her beauty, that our emotional and lovestruck Dante faints.

When he awakens, they proceed to the Tree of Knowledge together, where Beatrice issues him with a Divine Mission. He is to bring his journey and all that he has learned back to the land of the living, in service.

When we take a look back at the paths we have explored, those tied with the Golden Thread, it is here, at the end of every tradition, we encounter Wisdom. And, with our Wisdom, we too are issued a Divine Mission.

In the 12-Steps, the final 12th Step says, "Having had a spiritual awakening as the result of these steps, we tried to carry this message to alcoholics, and to practice these principles in all our affairs."

When we arrive in the North Lodge of the Medicine Wheel, we are to be in Service, to become the Elder with snowy white hair as white as the snows of the North, from a place of newfound Wisdom. And, since there is no end and no beginning to a Circle, we begin to travel the Wheel again. When we face the inevitable, we circumvent the Wheel again and again, each time gaining new Wisdom to bring into our world.

In Patanjali's Yoga Sutras, the light of intuitive wisdom lifts the veil of ignorance. We have reached Samadhi. From this place of being in the 'all and the nothing,' we become 'sage.'

And with every tradition or philosophy, we start our journey again, around the Circle, into deeper and more revealing realms. You will discover so many beautiful overlaps. Each shares the components of Wisdom and Service.

In this current state of our world, wisdom is sorely needed. However, before we can tackle the world, it begins with us first. We can learn much about cultivating wisdom from the contemplative practices, wisdom philosophers, and religious fundamentals.

In our quest for Wisdom, we all become philosophers. The two Greek words, 'philo' and 'sophia', from which our word 'philosophy' is derived, literally means lover of wisdom. One of the great Greek philosophers, Socrates, was the teacher of Plato, and had an eye-opening, early experience that founded the basis of all of his philosophy.

Socrates was told by the Oracle at Delphi that he was the wisest man in Athens. He couldn't understand how that could be true- even though he hungered for wisdom, he knew he didn't have it. There were lots of people in Athens who did regard themselves as wise. And Socrates sought them out. In the role of a student, eager to learn from his superiors, he set out to question the wise men of Athens. But he quickly discovered that despite the fact they all professed to be wise, none of them seemed to have a deep degree of wisdom. Most of them didn't seem to know anything at all. And that helped Socrates to finally understand what the Oracle had meant. At least he, Socrates, knew one thing to be true, that he wasn't wise.

Socrates is quoted as saying, *"True knowledge exists in knowing that you know nothing."*

And, I believe it to be true, that Wisdom can't be taught, it is something we gather experientially. The more we gather, the more we know that we simply do not know. How do we become Wise then?

It's not up to me, or anyone at this point in your pilgrimage, to teach you anything. You have the tools to explore this yourself, making this your own. You, through your own curiosity, study, exploration, and practice can cultivate the wisdom that becomes your Truth.

I will share though that nearing the end of one of many Dark Nights of the Soul, I found that the simple cultivation of curiosity and awe, inspired the continuation of my own practice. And this continues to lead me to deeper insights, each one more miraculous than the last.

In my daily life, regardless of circumstance, I am now practicing the following, and am finding it extremely challenging and worthwhile. I want to share it with you, even though I haven't mastered this yet, it continues to yield great promise for me.

Presence – Awareness Expansion Practice

I was seeking a way to bring my practices with me, into the everyday challenge of real life. It didn't seem practical to instantly meditate or do a Shamanic Journey. So, I created the following practice to try to bring more Mindfulness into my every breath.

Start small like while taking a walk, or washing dishes.
- Bring attention to your body, and 'turn on' your Presence (your inner awareness) as you do best.

- And, then begin to 'turn on' your outer Awareness at the same time, holding both in balance with the other.
- How much can you bring into your Awareness Field and still stay Present?

Even though it is only three steps, I found this extremely difficult at first. The key to this for me was to bring my inner Presence outward, as my sight, hearing, smell, and touch. Meaning, learn to listen with your body. Learn to see with your body. Learn to touch with your body. Learn to smell with your body. And, learn to 'be' with your body, rather than in my head with the steady stream of thought.

As this practice grew for me, I started to apply it to times in my life when I needed it most. For example, I hate to be rushed. So, when I would find myself in a hurry because traffic was running slower than I needed it to, I would always feel the sensation of nervousness by feeling rushed. I asked myself, could I be in a hurry, and not feel rushed? By bringing inner Presence into my outer world circumstance, I did find I could drive a little faster (within safe circumstances of course), or I could pick up the pace of my walk, and stay calm. And, if I couldn't control traffic, I could simply accept that and any consequences of it.

Could I face a shortage of money, without panicking?

Could I feel lonely, and not feel depressed and abandoned?

Could I be angry at my husband, and not hate him in that moment?

So many ways to bring inner Presence and outer Awareness together, and so much practice I have yet to do.

I believe Socrates to be very wise, in his knowing that he is not the master of all Wisdom and never will be. It is all a practice.

Because I know that I don't know, I've also only recently started to incorporate into my daily meditation a sense of complete receptivity. I started intentionally being open to receiving evolution, and that is when this book was born. Be prepared, once you fully open to the field of possibility, the circumstances in your life may drastically change. Stay in the fire of it, and you may be surprised as to what doors may open for you.

After Dante is taken through the Worlds of Paradise, he is ultimately taken to meet Mother Mary, and he is finally granted permission to see God.

O plenitude of grace, by which I could presume
To fix mine eyes upon eternal Light
Until my sight was spent on it!

In its depth I saw contained by love
Into a single volume bound, the pages
Scattered through the universe:

Substances, accidents, and the interplay
Between them, as though they were conflated
In such ways that what I tell is but a simple light.

In the deep, transparent essence of the lofty
Light there appeared to me three circles
Having three colors but the same extent,

And each one seemed reflected by the other
as rainbow is by rainbow, while the third seemed fire,
Equally breathed forth by one and by the other.

O how scant is speech, too weak to frame my thoughts.

O eternal Light, abiding in yourself alone,
knowing yourself
Alone, and, known to yourself and knowing,
Loving and smiling on yourself!

Here my exalted vision lost its power.

But now my will and my desire, like wheels

Revolving with an even motion, were turning
With the Love that moves the sun and all the other stars.
                    Dante's Paradiso, Canto XXXIII

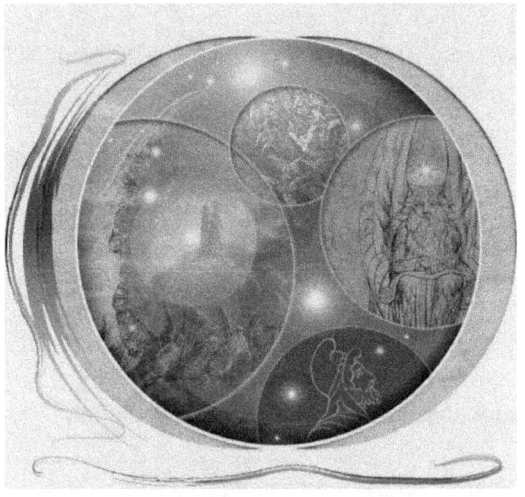

It's interesting to me that Dante describes the Universe as God made it, to be a place filled with the Light of Love, so bright that his sight was lost. With his Divine Sight, he continues to express what he sees as the deep, transparent essence. Three differently colored Circles appear, each reflected in the other, holographically, 'equally breathed forth by one and by the other'.

In the end, Dante's 'exalted vision' is taken away from him, and he is left to complete his mission of service. However, he is a reborn man, with balanced will and desire, being motivated by the same Universal Love that moves the sun and the stars.

It is here, my friend, that I too, take my leave, with very few words. I leave you in the eternal light of love in the Universe, within the same love that moves the sun and all other stars, where you can continue your journey of exploration with a much higher power than I.

Writing this book has been my own act of loving service to you, and its such a great honor that you have made it this far with me. I hope that my wanderings through the many portals and realms might scatter some breadcrumbs for you through your own dark forests. I can only hope that these words and practices might be able to help, if even one person, to navigate the great distance between Heaven and Hell, by following the Golden Thread laid by those who have gone before us.

And, once you've made it through the realms of discovery, that you can look back over the incredible journey you've just accomplished, to find that there never really was a Hell in the first place. It was all just a fantastic, epic adventure….

Journey on, my friend.

Appendix A - 12 Steps of AA

THE TWELVE STEPS OF ALCOHOLICS ANONYMOUS

1. We admitted we were powerless over alcohol—that our lives had become unmanageable.
2. Came to believe that a Power greater than ourselves could restore us to sanity.
3. Made a decision to turn our will and our lives over to the care of God as we understood Him.
4. Made a searching and fearless moral inventory of ourselves.
5. Admitted to God, to ourselves, and to another human being the exact nature of our wrongs.
6. Were entirely ready to have God remove all these defects of character.
7. Humbly asked Him to remove our shortcomings.
8. Made a list of all persons we had harmed, and became willing to make amends to them all.
9. Made direct amends to such people wherever possible, except when to do so would injure them or others.
10. Continued to take personal inventory and when we were wrong promptly admitted it.
11. Sought through prayer and meditation to improve our conscious contact with God as we understood Him, praying only for knowledge of His will for us and the power to carry that out.
12. Having had a spiritual awakening as the result of these steps, we tried to carry this message to alcoholics, and to practice these principles in all our affairs.

ILLUSTRATIONS
Paul Gustave Dor´e

Bibliography

"1867 English Translation by Longfellow." *Wikisource.Org*, Wikimedia Foundation, Inc., 21 Dec. 2017, en.wikisource.org/wiki/Divine_Comedy_(Longfellow_1867)/Volume_2. Accessed 25 Apr. 2019.

A Course in Miracles. Glen Elen, Ca, Foundation For Inner Peace, 1992.

Alighieri, Dante. *Inferno*. New York, Fall River Press, 2018.

---. *The Divine Comedy*. New York, Knopf, 1995.

Alighieri, Dante, and Charles Eliot Norton. *The Divine Comedy*. Stiwell, Ks, Digireads.Com, 2005.

Anonymous, Alcoholics. *Alcoholics Anonymous : The Story of How Many Thousands of Men and Women Have Recovered from Alcoholism*. New York City, Alcoholics Anonymous World Services, 2001.

Ardagh, Chameli. *Embodying the Feminine*. Awakening Women Institute, 2011.

Bear, Sun, et al. *Dancing with the Wheel : The Medicine Wheel Workbook*. New York, Simon & Schuster, 1992.

Campbell, Joseph. *The Hero with a Thousand Faces.* New York, Pantheon Books, 1968.

---. *The Power of Myth.* Place Of Publication Not Identified, Turtleback Books, 2012.

"Dante's Inferno." *Danteinferno.Info*, 2019, www.danteinferno.info/. Accessed 25 Apr. 2019.

Dreher, Diane. *The Tao of Inner Peace : A Guide to Inner and Outer Peace.* New York, N.Y., Harperperennial, 1991.

Hoffman, Dassie. *The Voice Dialogue Anthology : Explorations of the Psychology of Selves and the Aware Ego Process.* Albion, Calif., Delos, Inc, 2012.

Ingerman, Sandra. *Shamanic Journeying.* Boulder, Colo., Sounds True ; [Enfield, 2008.

Jung, C G. *Modern Man in Search of a Soul. Translated by W.S. Dell and Cary F. Baynes.* New York, Harcourt, Brace & World, 1973.

Longfellow, Henry. "1867 English Translation by Longfellow." *Wikisource.Org*, Wikimedia Foundation, Inc., 21 Dec. 2017, en.wikisource.org/wiki/Divine_Comedy_(Longfellow_1867)/Volume_2.

Rutherford, Leo. *View through the Medicine Wheel - Shamanic Maps of How the Universe Works.* John Hunt Publishing, 2008.

"SparkNotes: Inferno." *Sparknotes.Com*, 2019, www.sparknotes.com/poetry/inferno. Accessed 25 Apr. 2019.

Stone, Sidra. *The Shadow King.* Lincoln Iuniverse, 2000.

Tolle, Eckhart. *A New Earth : Awakening to Your Life's Purpose.* London], Uk Penguin Books, 2016.

---. *The Power of Now.* Vancouver, Namaste Pub, 2007.

Wikipedia Contributors. "Inferno (Dante)." *Wikipedia*, Wikimedia Foundation, 23 Apr. 2019, en.wikipedia.org/wiki/Inferno_(Dante). Accessed 25 Apr. 2019.

Wilber, Ken. *Integral Spirituality : A Startling New Role for Religion in the Modern and Postmodern World.* Boston, Mass., Integral Books, 2007.

www.ingramcontent.com/pod-product-compliance
Lightning Source LLC
Chambersburg PA
CBHW031444040426
42444CB00007B/956